Performance Anxiety

Also by Jonathan Lerner

Caught in a Still Place
Alex Underground
Swords in the Hands of Children
Lily Narcissus

With Joanna Brown, Barbara Lou Shafer, and Robert Anderson

Voices from Wounded Knee

Performance Anxiety

The Headlong Adolescence of a Mid-Century Kid

JONATHAN LERNER

RESOURCE *Publications* · Eugene, Oregon

PERFORMANCE ANXIETY
The Headlong Adolescence of a Mid-Century Kid

Resource Publications
An Imprint of Wipf and Stock Publishers
199 W. 8th Ave., Suite 3
Eugene, OR 97401

www.wipfandstock.com

PAPERBACK ISBN: 979-8-3852-2750-1
HARDCOVER ISBN: 979-8-3852-2751-8
EBOOK ISBN: 979-8-3852-2752-5

VERSION NUMBER 09/13/24

Dedicated to the memory of
Janet Axelrod

Contents

Houses and Cars | 1

Stress Hormones | 20

Cool Kids | 44

Chain Bridges | 64

Secret Passages | 90

1

Houses and Cars

I was sixteen as that year began. I had friends. I had fun. I liked my school. I smoked unfiltered Luckies. I reached my full height. I lost my virginity. I turned seventeen. That year I smoked pot for the first time. It was not a calendar year but a school year, 1964-65. That's when I was a senior in high school, and was given my first car. I came and went, as kids like me could freely do then, at mid-century. I was on the loose, growing up fast. As fast as I could if not as fast as I wished.

The car was purchased used that fall so I could drive myself from Chevy Chase, the Maryland suburb of Washington, D.C., where my family lived, into the city to Hawthorne, the small private school I attended. Though the car was in excellent condition, it cost my parents the now-laughable sum of $180. It was a 1956 Studebaker Commander. Studebaker made some sexy models, but this stodgy, upright sedan wasn't one of them. Still, as a kid, to have a car at my disposal, any car, at that moment in American history, a car essentially my own, reinforced the delusion that I (and the country) could do anything. The world was all for me (and us), ever-advancing, uninterruptible.

By mid-century here I mean the time, not the architecture and design. That era began perhaps unremarked, in the late forties, after the war—the war we won, unlike all the wars since. I was born in 1948, at the peak of the baby boom. The baby boom was a demographic phenomenon that must have seemed curious, if benign, until my enormous generation grew old enough for our disruptive potential to emerge. The upheavals of the sixties and seventies marked the mid-century period's ragged close. My childhood, adolescence, and early adulthood all took place within that time. You might call me Mid-Century Man. I'm thinking of myself more as a mid-century kid.

The beckoning ribbons of the Interstate Highway system were just then being unrolled across the landscape. The postwar economic boom was racing ahead at full speed. The social contract and the public institutions that supported it still appeared intact. The forecast was endless and sunny—for white people like me who weren't poor. But wait! Civil rights legislation was being enacted, even! And in 1964, the Vietnam War was still only a faint rumbling from a great distance. The counterculture's creative destruction had barely commenced. The annual summertime heatwave of conflagrations in Black urban communities didn't become widespread until the following year. There had only been a couple of newsworthy assassinations, those of Medgar Evers and some other civil rights activists, and JFK's. And if the former were largely ignored, the latter seems in retrospect to have elicited a broad collective anguish, bringing people together; the polarizing conspiracy theories and culture wars to come were unimagined. I locate America's imperial high point in 1964, and believe it's been downhill ever since.

Or maybe I spotlight 1964 in this way just because that's when I got my driver's license and first car.

The Studebaker was painted in an assertive color called Air Force Blue Metallic. It had a throaty Sweepstakes 259 V8 engine. In this car I did most of what an insecure but cocky teenaged boy will do when furnished with wheels: driving as acting out. I was reckless. I had numerous small accidents and scrapes. I got tickets. I drove drunk, with four or five equally drunk friends piled in—it was a big car with bench seats front and back. I handled that piece of heavy machinery blithely, as if there were never any danger, or as if it paradoxically served as armor against danger, and it's lucky nobody got hurt. What I did not ever do in that car was have sex. I was having sex by then, just not in the car. As far as I was concerned sex, too, was danger-free, and if the people I was having it with got hurt I didn't notice. The girls I was having it with, I mean. Forcing myself to have it with, I mean. In 1964, I was troubled by but still long years away from embracing the fact that I am gay.

At the end of that school year the Hawthorne senior class—all forty-eight of us—made a study trip to Charlottesville, Virginia. I drove, in the Commander, with several classmates along. It was a beautiful June day. The windows were down, the radio blaring. I felt an offhand confidence in my future, an offhand fondness for the kids riding with me. We were singing along at the top of our lungs, to "The In Crowd."

The theme of the trip to Charlottesville was Thomas Jefferson as designer. We toured his estate Monticello, where there was no mention I can recall of slaves, and visited the university campus he designed. Toward dusk, we caravanned up the rutted allee of a defunct plantation called Bremo. The designer of its big house had worked with Jefferson on Monticello. At Bremo, the slave quarters were dilapidated but standing. As evening came on, I had one of the few mystical experiences of my life while not on drugs, watching silent ghosts come and go through the quarters' crumbling walls.

Six months earlier, on another dreamlike weekday afternoon, the school office got a call from my father. I was pulled out of class. Minutes later I was behind the wheel. "Always Something There to Remind Me" was on the radio. I was heading to George Washington University Hospital. My mother was there, in a room, in a bed, in a coma, dying of metastatic breast cancer.

* * *

But there is rarely something there to remind me.

I have only an antique table she bought, a pair of candlesticks, and a lamp. There is also a scrapbook of letters she wrote home to her closest friends from Taiwan, where we lived in the late fifties during my father's first Foreign Service posting. Mom's letters reveal her as perceptive and empathic. She had a wry sense of humor, and could tell a vivid story. The letters are certainly in her voice, in the literary sense. They express her sensibilities and distinctive turns of phrase. She used descriptors like "darling" and "stunning." Sometimes she sprinkled in jazzy anachronisms, like "at the mo'" and "natch," and Yiddish-accented expressions like "to you I wouldn't lie." What she wrote is mediated—defused emotionally—by being ink on paper, visual and static. I can control how I take it in. Skip around, reread, pause to ponder a locution, or to envision a scene.

There is also a recorded conversation of us as a family, made in Taipei when I was ten. Hearing her speak on that tape is painful in a way that reading her letters is not. The tape delivers her words uninterrupted and at her own tempo, with the actual sound of her voice. I can very clearly recall the sound of many other people speaking, even the voices of people I have not spoken with during the many decades my mother has been dead. But hers I cannot conjure up. I have listened to this recording many times. There might still be cells in the auditory cortex of my brain that were imprinted with her voice from infancy. But the sound of it always startles me with its unfamiliarity. I am surprised every time that she has a distinct Eastern Pennsylvania accent. I am surprised at the softness, the hum, of her speech.

I was aware that her cancer was terminal. My father had told me six months or so before she died. This does not mean I was prepared for her death. He had also told my sister Marcia and my brother Steve, who were twenty-two and twenty, around the same time as he told me. When I left the hospital a few minutes after Mom died it was because Daddy sent me home to be there when our younger brother Higgy, aged twelve, came from school. It was my job, at sixteen, to tell him. Higgy was the only immediate family member whom no one had thought to have with us that afternoon at the hospital. Higgy was also the only one of us kids who had not been forewarned. Well, Daddy told him the night before—does that count? At least Marcia, Steve and I had known for a while, though we were each alone with the information. Nobody made an attempt to talk about it and, as far as anybody remembers, Mom herself never uttered the word cancer. I told a few of my friends, for the glamour of impending personal tragedy, not as if it would prompt me to process the fact, or because I hoped it would start helpful conversations. And what would they have known to say?

My mother's parents, Ida and Louie, had also been kept from knowing about her decade-long fight with the disease. Years later, a friend of my mother's told me that Mom didn't want to tell them because she expected that her own mother would swoop in and start bossing her around. My grandparents' obliviousness was also possibly effectuated by their reluctance to recognize the obvious over the years of Mom's illness. They were only told a few days before the end. They were with us at the hospital when she died, along our family friends Kathy and Mike Birnbaum. Mike, unusually for that time, wore a beard. Somebody later said that his beard, and his fluency in Yiddish, suggested to Ida and Louie the presence of a rabbi, so was a comfort. Who knows?

Within hours my grandparents were fed tranquilizers and put on a flight home to Florida. Later that evening, a dozen close friends, people who had been like aunts and uncles to us all our lives, and a few nearby relatives, came over for coffee and murmured condolences. That was it for support. There was no funeral. Several of those friends, years later, told me how shocked they had been at the lack of ceremony. They thought my father was doing it all wrong. But people didn't presume to correct even close friends' parenting then, and maybe still don't.

Daddy was in charge, and he was not thinking of how we might be handling the loss. No doubt he was exhausted from Mom's long downward spiral. He also had a big secret. He was in love with Kathy, and they were already planning to marry. I suppose he must have been focused on his imagined future. He wanted to move on quickly and he made no space for us kids to grieve, or even talk. This reflected a well-entrenched culture of avoiding uncomfortable topics. So we each had to reckon with Mom's death alone. We took a day off school, and then he announced, "OK, business as usual tomorrow."

I said above "my mother has been dead." At least I can say it. When she died, and long afterwards, I could only refer to her absence by indirection. I borrowed the formulation I needed from a girl in my class at Hawthorne School. Luckily for me, if unluckily for her, she was an orphan. When people asked about her family, she would say, with what to me was enviable poise, "My parents aren't living." I could manage that. My mother wasn't living. I had not been invited to mourn, and this was more not-mourning. I succeeded at not-mourning until I was just the age Mom was at death, a few weeks shy of fifty, when I received a diagnosis of depression. And having been instructed so early, and so well, in not-mourning, I still have trouble letting myself react when people close to me die. It's too bad, now that I've reached the age when it seems that every couple of weeks someone I know is changing planes for their final destination.

* * *

I can't have been older than three or so because Abe, my father, was carrying me. We were in a hardware store. I was enjoying an unaccustomed high vantage point from my father's arms. And I was absorbed in watching the activity: men coming and going, asking for help, being helped, chatting. Someone called out, "Oh, Mr. Johnson—" and I swiveled around to look over Daddy's shoulder, and answered, "What?" All the guys went, "Ha ha." Mr. Johnson thus became my nickname, mostly used by Abe, my father, fondly, and still now occasionally by my sister, Marcia.

It is uncomfortable even now to write "my father's arms" and "my father, fondly." Late in his life our relationship was warmer. But when I was a kid what I felt from him was mostly incomprehension, or indifference. Or exasperation. Now I think the awkwardness was mutual, and wonder where it came from. The prickle of small wounds, perhaps, reciprocally inflicted and selectively hoarded.

But mutual: After he died, my stepmother told me he'd once said that when I was small I didn't want him to touch me.

The other day I found an old crinkle-edged snapshot of the two of us. We are sitting on a stone retaining wall in front of a boarding house in Atlantic City, New Jersey, where we went sometimes in the summer, to get away from the Washington heat. That was pre-highrise, pre-casino, pre-utterly-blasted-and-cored-out-by-racism-and-greed Atlantic City. I think the photo was taken in 1950, the summer when I was two. Daddy has me snugged against him, with his arm around me. I am dolled up in a pair of what I believe are called "suspender shorts," with a crisp white shirt and, inexplicably for a beach town in summer, a bow tie. I appear to be rigid, almost grimacing, hands clamped between my knees, looking off obliquely. Daddy seems relaxed––he's saying something to whoever holds the camera. In the background, hanging on the railing of the boarding house porch, so that it's right next to my father's head in the photo, is a sign that says "Vacancy." Also, everything in the picture is slightly out of focus.

In Lynne Tillman's novel *Men and Apparitions* an anthropologist obsessively studying his own family's photographs declares, "Pictures become a memory for which you have no actual memory." But even though I have been holding its photographic evidence in my hand and staring at it repeatedly for days, I still don't remember the moment in this snapshot. I can't even pretend a memory of it. I do recall another incident from that same Atlantic City vacation, of which there is no photo. Our maid Maggie had been brought along to mind us kids. One day she took my brother Steve and me for a promenade along the boardwalk. I was in my stroller. Steve, who was six at the time, was pushing it. He is not in fact the rebel of the family—that would turn out to be my calling—so this was somewhat out of character, but he was seized with the idea of making a break for it. Propelling me ahead of him, he ran away, with Maggie chasing after us. I wonder how Maggie felt, as perhaps the only Black person in sight, running after two little white kids. But I don't suppose it would have struck bystanders as too odd because they would have been used to seeing white kids in the care of Black women. In my mind's eye, Steve and I are giddy with the thrill of escape, Maggie's skirts are flying, and it took her the length of several city blocks to catch up to us, breathless. But can I possibly remember this event? Or is it an example of a different process of confabulation: *Stories* become a memory for which you have no actual memory. This is a story I heard told and retold. Did my mental picture originate in hearing the incident described? This "memory" is not just a snapshot in time, either. Like a story, it's an action sequence, a motion picture: wind whipping and skirts flying and even, if I pull the camera back, gulls wheeling overhead and breakers rolling onto the beach below.

This is a caution: Even I don't know for sure how much of what I'm writing is "true," especially anecdotes like these from when I was so young. What about the incident in the hardware store? It happened for sure, because my father witnessed it and told it, and it produced an artifact in the form of a nickname though not a photo. But surely much of the visual detail I "remember" has been filled in after the fact: a guy behind the counter helping out a customer, and the wall behind him with its pigeon holes full of different screws and bolts, even that it was my father's right shoulder I was looking over. It's a good story, though, and a pleasant "memory." Though sometimes remembered stories are not so good.

I can't help but read that "Vacancy" sign over my father's shoulder in Atlantic City as an accidental metaphor. I'm studying two other photos of him. I can't remember their moments because both were taken before I was born. But I keep looking at them because they reiterate a feeling of emptiness. Surely that is coincidental. Bad lighting, wrong exposure, fuzzy focus: many things can render a harmlessly intended picture disturbing.

One is an exterior shot, in winter. Behind Abe you can see a small tree with bare branches, and the white clapboard side of some house. He is facing the camera in a buttoned-up trench coat, his hands clasped behind his back. Another man standing next to him is mostly out of the frame so we only see his coat sleeve, his shoulder, and a slice of his hat brim. It must have been a sunny midday, because my father's fedora casts a dark shadow across his forehead and eyes, while from the bridge of his nose downward his face is illuminated. But the whole picture looks bleached out. Overexposed? Maybe it's just faded; the print is at least eighty years old. I took a magnifying glass to it, to try to make out my father's eyes, but there is, as the term of art in this era of digital imagery would have it, no information there.

The other photo, in the margin of which is penned "1945" in his unmistakable hand, is of Daddy at his desk, in suit and tie, holding a pipe in his mouth. Sunlight floods through a window to his right so that half of the picture is almost entirely blown out. There are just faint outlines for his desk top, his entire right side, the piece of paper he is holding up. The intense light also blanks out his eyeglasses. I can see his brows above the frames, but whatever was behind the lenses is missing.

* * *

My mother had some strong quality that drew other women close—just like sisters, more than one of them later said to me. Mom's name, long now out of fashion, was Elsie. Among her women friends were Claire, Marian, Ruth, Edith, Ethel, Evelyn, Annette, Gertrude, and Sylvia who was called Cissy. Some of those names sound antiquated now, too. ("Cissy" was odd for me when I was very young, since in our household lingo to "make a sissy" was to pee. It was differently troubling when I was a little older and understood that being called a sissy meant you were a fraidy cat. Later still, as a teen, I learned that sissy also meant faggot. But by then I knew about homonyms and no longer associated the word sissy with our family friend Cissy who was like a sister to my mother and like an aunt to us kids.)

Mom had a cousin named Pearl. We called her Pearlie. Mom was maybe ten years older, but they were very close growing up. We kids naturally loved Pearlie because we could see the resemblance between her and our mother, and she was warm to us, a great big hugger. Leonard, her husband, we loved too. While Pearlie, like Mom, was curvy, he was wiry. Leonard was a real cutup, a card. He had flailed around trying to make a living. For a while, when they lived in rural South Jersey, he drove a truck hauling potatoes for farmers. Finally he acquired a clothing shop, in a town north of Philadelphia.

Len's Mens and Boys was a small-town, Main-Street business just when retail was abandoning Main Streets for suburban strips. One summer I "worked" there for a week, or maybe a day, twiddling my thumbs mostly when I wasn't admiring the stacks of neatly folded and pinned shirts, considering which might end up in my back-to-school wardrobe. I was twelve, conscious even then of presentation. I didn't really know Len well. But I was charmed by his playfulness, by his youth relative to my own parents, and felt secure in our family connection. Not much was happening on that particular Main Street, and idle pals of Len's would stop by to kibitz. That summer, civil rights protests were on TV all the time. I was gripped, and inspired, and naive enough to assume that since my parents and their friends were liberals and against segregation, everyone else we knew must have been, too. So it was a shock to hear Len and his pals toss around racist jests and slanders when discussing the news. Lenny was racist! I never felt comfortable around him again.

But how racist? At that age I just saw good and bad. It was not until after I had spent most of my twenties in a doctrinaire leftist cult, the Weathermen, that I began to grasp the subtleties of where attitudes come from, how they're nuanced, and evolve, or don't. In Len's shop I was self-conscious and debilitated in the company of those grown men. Something challenging, belittling, invisible, but woozy-making, wafted off them in my direction. It was an ephemeral trace, I see now, of the testing that men typically present to one another when they meet—just a reflex emanation, though. I would hardly have registered to them at all, and certainly not as any threat. But they felt like a threat to me.

How easily my assumption of safety could shatter. As a young child, encounters might have been enchanting or unsettling, crystalline or unintelligible. The world was prismatic and unpredictable, but stable and mostly entertaining. It didn't need to make sense. Now there was twelve-year-old me, on the wobbly ladder of adolescence.

One shirt I took home from Len's that summer was a yellow and green, Madras-plaid button-down, very smart. My innocence was just then being inundated by my approach into puberty, by my own body's trickle of changes. And I was drowning in the hormonal miasma of a suburban junior high school with two thousand teenage students. How was I to know that wearing green and yellow on a Thursday was mysteriously but universally understood by all other boys to be positive proof that one was a homo? I was just trying to dress nicely—and keep secret, from myself and everybody else, that indeed I might be one. As if dressing nicely would disguise it.

* * *

Like Elsie, the name Pearl seems old fashioned now, along with so many other names that are names of jewels. Including the name Jewel itself. That's what I called a character in a novel I didn't finish. It makes me a little sad that since I didn't, I'll never know how things turned out for her. She was of my mother's generation, and like Mom somebody who got things done. But she was prickly and aloof, not surrounded by women friends. Although she was a lesbian. Jewel, my invention, I mean.

I did once meet a Garnet, when I was in my thirties. She grew up—or I should say wised up—in the Mississippi Delta in the years when civil rights organizers were being attacked and murdered there. She was a white girl who became an activist of the anti-racist and radical-feminist sort, and a criminal defense attorney. She drove around with a gun in the glove compartment, which impressed me enormously.

Beryl is a mineral with many differently colored varieties, some being gemstones. I did know a girl called Berry, which must have been short for Beryl. We were in a Hebrew-school carpool on Tuesdays and Thursdays when junior high let out—Thursdays, when I tried not to forget and wear that green-and-yellow shirt. I did forget, several times, to the general entertainment of the

11

mean boys. Perhaps I was acting on subconscious impulse when I dressed dangerously. A brave but erroneous interpretation would be that I was flying a green-and-yellow flag on purpose to announce that I was queer, long before the rainbow took on that meaning. I don't know why I wore that shirt on Thursdays. But what's objectively true is that in doing so, just when incipient adolescence was challenging me to project some shred of sexual self-confidence, in an environment that allowed it only one expression, I sabotaged the effort.

Like Jewel in my unfinished novel, the only Sapphire I ever knew of was a character in fiction: Sapphire Stevens, in the TV show "Amos 'n' Andy." This was a situation comedy descended from the minstrel show tradition, the only program on early television with an all-Black cast. It aired in 1951, 1952, and 1953, when I was three, four, and five. The title characters, who were respectively naive and gullible, ran a taxi company. Sapphire was married to their friend Kingfish who constantly tried to involve them in preposterous schemes, at which Sapphire would roll her eyes. Maybe "Amos 'n' Andy" was all just shuckin' and jivin' racist caricature. It did offer a window into a different world which we then called colored, or Negro. It depicted Black people as human, and warm, and funny. I especially loved Sapphire, who was simultaneously spunky and long-suffering. During those same years I, along with several other white children, was driven to nursery school on days when nobody's mother was available, in a royal blue Chrysler limousine by a Black man named Mr. Hatton. Mr. Hatton wore the same kind of driver's cap as Amos and Andy. And his name included the word hat! This was confusing. But in contrast to those two, Mr. Hatton was rather courtly, and he was not trying to entertain us children. He may have been performing, but he was hardly playing for laughs—talking about Black people as human.

It occurred to me that lots of drag queens must have come up with names suggesting glitter, as in jewels. Surprisingly, online lists of drag names, of which there are many, turn up very few such concoctions. Pearl Pendant, Ruby Slippers: Meh. These hardly exude the bitter acid of high drag humor. It was fun reading the lists though. I got a kick out of Ida Slapter. And what can you even say about Frieda Slaves?

I can't recall ever having met an Opal. But that's what I somehow couldn't stop calling a little neighbor girl I know now whose name is Iris, a flower. I've known several people named for flowers. I crossed paths once as a child with a girl named Daisy. She was the first colored, or Negro, pupil in my second grade class, in 1955, when our schools were integrated following Brown v Board of Education. Daisy had many little braids, which seemed odd to me at the time because I hadn't ever been close enough to any Black girls to be familiar with their styles of braids. The familiar braids were on the girl who sat in front of me, Margaret (a name, incidentally, which derives from the Greek for pearl). Margaret's braids were blond and numbered only two. She was from South Africa, and spoke with a clipped accent as exotic as Daisy's braids. She told me, unforgettably, that she pictured her stomach as a chamber containing a pile of food and a pile of fingernail fragments she'd bitten off and swallowed. I don't remember Daisy's voice at all, nor anything she might have said. It seems to me she was very quiet. Maybe she was a chatterbox at home, but it must have been stupefyingly lonely, even frightening, to be the only Black kid in class.

The one Black person I knew intimately as a child was also named for a flower. Violet Seawall was our family's maid. This was after Maggie of the boardwalk breakout attempt had left us, but when I was still quite small. I loved Violet madly. Violet married a man named Joseph Washington. I did like the dignified sound of Violet Seawall Washington. Possibly because we lived in suburban Washington, I often thought of George Washington as alive and present and looking over my shoulder. I didn't know then that many people with the surname Washington are descended from slaves who had been the property of George and Martha Washington. With her new last name Washington, I expected Violet to remain a presence too, but I don't believe I ever saw her again after she married Joseph, and I was bereft.

My family had other Black maids, besides Maggie and Violet, not named for flowers. There was Rebecca, and also Beulah.

No, wait. "Beulah" was another early-fifties TV show, about a Black maid working for a white family. It was also a comedy, with the joke usually being on Beulah, which added to the impression that people of color existed for our amusement. Beulah was also the name my parents' friends Virginia and Tony gave to their tanklike Plymouth coupe, vintage 1948, in which they were still rumbling around ten years later when every other family I knew drove a newer car, since cars were crap and generally fell apart fast back then. Tony was a Jewish Czech immigrant, a geographer who taught at historically Black Howard University. He had perhaps a survivor's frugality. He and Virginia lived in a duplex, a two-family house, and in D.C., not in a single-family house on a big suburban lot like ours. I found Tony rather remote. But I liked his wit. My father had been the president of our synagogue. Throughout my childhood whenever Tony called he would always ask whoever picked up the phone, in his debonair Czech accent, "Have I reached the White House? Is the President at home?" Speaking of George Washington.

Actually the Washingtons, George and Martha, never occupied the White House. It was under construction, largely through the labor of enslaved Black men, while he was President. But they were present in our house, in my imagination. His profile was and still is embossed on the quarter, where he looks ruggedly handsome, perhaps more so than was true. It intrigued me as a child that on the quarter he had long hair gathered in a queue, while in those years men, the ones I knew anyway, wore theirs in military brush cuts or oiled and tamed. I caught this glimpse of George frequently, the quarter being a unit of money with which I was certainly familiar. I don't remember at what age I started being given a weekly allowance—seven? eight?—but I know it was a quarter. By the time I was being fag-baited in junior high, the price of a coke at the Drug Fair soda fountain where I stopped on my way home from school had risen to fifteen cents. The Black women who served at the soda fountain—it was always Black women serving in places like that, around Washington then—made each one up individually. A squeeze of Coke syrup, a blast of carbonated water.

You could customize yours with a second syrup, for a cherry Coke or, my favorite, a vanilla Coke. That brought the price up to twenty. I'd like to think I just routinely left a quarter, with the extra nickel as a tip. But perhaps I did not.

Martha Washington played a lesser role in my imagination than her husband, though I also had a mental image of her based on a physical token. It wasn't really meant to be her. Cheap sewing kits have, or used to have, a metal needle threader the handle of which was impressed with the silhouette of an old-fashioned lady. Stamped in relief on a flat metal object of roughly the same scale, it seemed an adequate mate for George's likeness on the quarter. That this female image was shallow and generic, the needle threader thin and flimsy—woman, pliant and blurred—did not make me wonder. George on the quarter was the firm and dimensional person, the embodiment of history to whom I assigned identity, however cartoonishly. He was like Scrooge McDuck, also rich, or Superman, also a hero. George Washington was a benevolent presence whose approval I longed for. When new and modern inventions impressed me, such as power windows and air conditioning in cars, I would long to show them off to George Washington. Both features were quite uncommon then; our own cars certainly didn't have them. But I felt proud of them, American achievements as fabulous as skyscrapers, and planes that could land on water, and atom bombs. I thought, Wouldn't George Washington be impressed by power windows and air conditioning in cars? I didn't stop to think that cars alone would give him pause.

* * *

In the course of my childhood, we lived in three different houses in Chevy Chase. Mom had the real estate itch. From when I was seven until I was fourteen, except for our two years in Taipei, we had a big shingled Victorian house that was marvelous to be a kid in. It had window seats to curl up reading in, and sliding pocket doors between the parlors that we kids used like curtains when we made up plays for audiences of visiting friends and relations. On the third floor, off Steve's room, there was a balcony from which to lob water balloons and snowballs at passersby. And there were secret passages and hidden spaces under the eaves. It was located on Drummond Avenue, in the old part of Chevy Chase, close to the District Line which separates Maryland from D.C. Our single street had been quaintly, all by itself, incorporated as the Village of Drummond in 1916, the year our house there went up.

When my parents bought that house they got eye rolls from their friends. Though it had plenty of character and space—seven bedrooms, in fact—it was old and unwieldy and needed work. But Daddy was descended from a line of carpenters, and could do a lot of the work himself. In fact, for a while before he went to work for the government, he himself had a construction business. Lerner Homes Corporation put up a small post-war subdivision of dinky houses, in Prince George's County, abetted by the no-down-payment mortgages available to veterans (Negroes excepted).

Daddy's construction site was always referred to as "the job." In another indirect benefit of the war, he had bought for little money an Army-surplus Jeep to use at the job. He once used it to tow us kids on a sled across a snowy meadow—Marcia, Steve and me, that is; this was before Higgy was born, so I can't have been older than barely four. That was the sort of family fun nobody thought twice about back then but which danger-averse parents of today would never dare. Alas, Daddy's construction company failed due, the story went, to materials shortages caused by the Korean War. But many years later when I paid a visit to my parents' close friends Claire and Joe, Claire said, "Abe Lerner is the only person I know who didn't make a fortune in Washington real estate, because he was too damn honest. If a sidewalk was uneven, he would rip it out and do it over."

Among his many projects at Drummond Avenue, one was hardly essential. In our back yard, he built us boys a remarkable tree house. It was about a dozen feet off the ground, a deck eight feet square with the trunk of the enormous oak that supported it rising right through the middle. A rope ladder could be drawn up through a trap door, to prevent unauthorized entry by enemy neighborhood children. There was a pail and pulley arrangement, anchored at its far end next to the kitchen door, by which snacks could be hauled in. Now as I tell these things, Abe seems a nicer guy and more engaged dad than I remember. I could perhaps cut him some slack.

Up on the third floor, behind a cupboard door in the wall of Steve's bedroom, among other detritus in one of those under-the-eaves spaces which a kid could crawl through from one room to another, was stored a roll of blueprints. During the period of my father's building business, when things were looking good it must have been, my parents commissioned an architect to design a house for them. They owned a building lot in a new neighborhood near Rock Creek Park where a number of their friends did eventually put up stylish modern houses. I don't remember much about the house depicted in the blueprints except that it was to have had a screened porch across the back. And Mom said it would have had silent radiant heating in the floors, which sounded like some kind of magic; we were used to radiators that clanked and hissed. The money went away or maybe never existed in the first place, the project was abandoned and the lot sold.

I believe this house that never was became a source of vague yearning for my mother, as it did for me. I got a similar wistful feeling when I looked at photographs of Abe's parents; I never knew his father, and his mother died when I was two. Of her I have only a couple of static, sketchy, maybe-memories—her homemade rose-petal jam, and her maroon late-forties Dodge—and glimpses of her from a few snapshots. These images and memory fragments evoked a longing for things I might once have had, or that I ought to have had, vague things I vaguely felt should have been mine. But having mentioned both the rose-petal jam and the maroon Dodge in the same sentence, I am now suspicious. It's perhaps too coincidental that both the jam and the car would have been exactly the same color. Come to think of it, there was a comforter in our house when I was little that was also that color. This is confusing. We called it "the quilt," although technically it wasn't one. It was covered in satin, or some satiny fabric. I always assumed it came from this grandmother. I do remember her being sick at our house, and always thought she died there but my older siblings say not. The comforter was a sort of collective possession, passed around and used mostly when one of us was sick and needed, well, comfort. Wrapping up in it felt like a grandmotherly embrace.

Besides the house near Rock Creek Park that was never built, there was another possibility for a unique house. This would have been after the failure of Lerner Homes Corporation but before we moved to the Victorian on Drummond Avenue. At the time, when I was about six, we were living in a decent but conventional house of the center-hall Colonial style. My parents—or, surely, my mother, who was always looking—came across a disused machine shop for sale. Decades before the rage for industrial-to-residential conversions, it seems that my parents toyed with the idea of turning this shell into a house for us. "Machine shop" was an enchanting description to me, suggesting fantastic contraptions: flywheels and cogs, racketing engines, shrill steam whistles. In fact it was silent, just a big, empty space with concrete floors, exposed steel girders, and huge metal-framed windows. This plan never materialized, for reasons also probably financial.

My parents' friends—the professionals and business owners among them, not the civil servants like Daddy whose incomes were more or less fixed—were flourishing in those boom years. Many of them became rich enough to build new houses in contemporary style with all the latest conveniences. Our Drummond Avenue house was singular, and pretty fabulous, but it wasn't fashionable or modern; the Victorian aesthetic was out and would not soon come back in. My mother still longed for something else. Perhaps this house didn't satisfy her need to keep up appearances, or to keep up with her friends.

Now, she was hardly just a housewife. She had a series of jobs. She sold real estate. She attempted a couple of creative business schemes which were house-oriented, too, though neither got off the ground: importing a line of furniture, contemporary interpretations of traditional Chinese forms, from Taiwan; restoring a run-down Dupont Circle townhouse, long before gentrification, and house flipping, and a return to city centers were named trends. In her final years she worked as secretary to the principal of an elementary school. But in the culture of that era being a homemaker was the normative and valued form of expression for a woman. Maybe she felt that our shaggy Victorian house somehow reflected on her poorly. Or perhaps she'd just had it with the skimpy closets, the too-few bathrooms and the clanky radiators. She started spending Sunday afternoons touring for-sale open houses, modern houses mostly, most newly built. In those boom years, with the suburbs spreading like a stain, there were always plenty of them to visit. I often went with her.

I was away at summer camp when she noticed that an intriguing house within our means was on the market. I didn't have the chance to resent not being consulted on the decision to buy it, because it was a done deal by the time I got home at the end of August, and we moved the following week. And I loved it. The house had been designed in the International Style by a German immigrant architect who had trained at the Bauhaus. It was cubic, flat-roofed, unornamented, and machine-like, in Corbusier's sense of "a machine for living." It had been commissioned by a classical pianist, and for acoustic purposes it had a two-story living room surrounded by a second-floor gallery, which gave it big drama. An intervening owner had been Marquis Childs, a now-forgotten but then-prominent journalist and liberal political commentator. Mom had been inside the house once, to a tea given by Mrs. Childs, and it had made a lasting impression. The house had provenance and panache. There was no other quite like it anywhere around. It satisfied my mother's craving for a remarkable home. She got to live in it for twenty-seven months before she died.

2

Stress Hormones

A t that center-hall Colonial we lived in before the Victorian on Drummond Avenue, the family next door included a boy my age whom I'll call Edmund Laughlin. One day, when Edmund and I were four or five years old, we were playing in his back yard. The grass there had been allowed to grow so long that rolling around in it gave the sensation of being caressed. Which one of us thought it would be even more pleasurable if we got naked? This might technically be my earliest experience of homoeroticism. It was entirely innocent. It may have been sex of a sort, but it was also just play. We were interrupted when his family's Irish maid leaned out an upstairs window and yelled, "Dir-ty! Dir-ty! Edmund Laughlin! Come inside this instant!"

I just thought it was funny, how the Irish maid got so mad, and how she pronounced "dir-ty." This experience did not imprint on me the idea that naked play with boys was sick. I got that message later. But I'm pretty sure that Edmund was not allowed to play with me again. And I did grasp that this activity should not be conducted out in the open. In the next years there were several other little boys whom, had we been adults, I might be referring to here as fuck buddies. We played our games in attics, under stairs, out in the woods. Hiding our naked play only added to the fun. As an adolescent and young adult, my earliest, unequivocally homosexual encounters were also suffused with secrecy. Even later, after Stonewall and the efflorescence of gay liberation, much of the sex I (and many other gay men) had was also anonymous, if not entirely covert. Possibly all little boys love hiding places, or maybe that's only those who are queer. But are we all—gay men—as I have been, drawn to secrets, and secret sex, even when we are more or less grown up?

By the time I was in junior high school, conflicted about and mildly bullied for being a homo, I was miserable a lot of the time. I was not athletic and hated being forced to play sports. In gym class I was called spaz and fag, and then obliged to shower naked with dozens of other boys, risking further trouble by not being able to avert my eyes from their vigorous gleaming bodies—and more dangerously, from their genitalia. Not all of them were irresistible. Some were flabby or scrawny. I wasn't the only awkward one. Memory, however, has erased all but the self-satisfied and the beautiful. One outcome of a successful passage through adolescence is sexual awareness and a modicum, at least, of sexual confidence. I had skipped fifth grade while we lived in Taipei. When we returned to Washington and I first found myself in the testosterone-saturated junior-high environment I was only eleven, and not even prepubescent. My consciousness of sexuality was still vague. At first I regarded at those boys in the shower with curiosity more than lust. I could hardly acknowledge my own germinal desires, or envision the acts they might lead to. No doubt all the boys in junior high were more or less both obsessed with and confounded by sex; it wasn't just a challenge for the late bloomers and the queers. But the pervasive homophobia-by-default made it seem as if I had nothing in common with the rest of them, as if they all belonged to a fraternity I would never be invited to join.

Then puberty arrived, marking the end of being oblivious of and untroubled by sex. Now I began to feel inchoate pangs of desire for other guys. This was a longing for romance, for passion and intimacy, quite different than that frolicking with little boys. I still knew enough to keep these impulses hidden; now I realized they could provoke condemnation and even violence. The thrill of secrecy was now interlaced with panic. Sex, obviously, was no longer a harmless game. It wasn't until I was an adult, when there was finally an open, proud queer community and political movement—even though I still didn't come out as gay for years after that—that fear ceased to be a routine factor in my homosexual encounters.

By the time I reached puberty I also understood that, in a culture that offered no alternative to being "normal," I was supposed to be getting interested in girls, not just as friends but as girlfriends. What I didn't quite get was that I was supposed to be interested in them sexually. I surely knew it in theory, but I could hardly have imagined sex with a girl then. I suppose at moments I could see myself, in soft focus, chastely embracing another kid, girl or boy: bare shoulders visible maybe, but the rest of the picture vague, smudged like a charcoal sketch and losing detail toward its margins. Of course, it was the rare kid who at that age was actually having sex. That was the case not just for the homos but also for the straight ones, even those who openly claimed they were "going steady" or "in love."

On Friday afternoons in the junior high school gym there was sometimes an informal "Coke dance." And there were two or three bigger-deal dances every year on Saturday nights, the same drab gym feebly decorated with crepe paper streamers. I attended all these and danced with girls. But it was the dancing I liked, and it wouldn't have occurred to me—it was unimaginable because impossible—to dance with boys. Anyway this was the dawning era of the Twist, the Mashed Potato, the Pony and all those rock-and-roll dances performed with a partner but without touching. That suited me well enough. There would always be a few traditional slow dances, too, set to romantic ballads—the boy, leading, one hand on a girl's hip and she, following, one on his shoulder. In those dances I didn't mind this ritualized and rigid physical contact, but was mainly nervous about whether I was placing my feet correctly as we performed the steps.

By ninth grade I'd become friends with a girl I'll call Carolyn. She was unrestrained, kooky, a lot of fun. I had a crush on her, or I told myself she was somebody I should have a crush on. Certain days after school we would take a bus together down to Georgetown, the most urbane neighborhood of Washington, which was then a rather sleepy and provincial town. She went to take modern dance classes, and for a while, to enjoy her company, I took that class, too. Lots of girls took ballet or modern dance lessons, whether they had any serious interest in it or not. As a general rule, boys did not. Carolyn said the real reason she went was to hear the Black woman named Jean who improvised fantastic jazz accompaniment on the piano. So I said the same. Jean's music really was remarkable. And I did like the physical discipline, not that I was serious about dance. Sometimes on the way to class Carolyn and I would stroll through Georgetown, browsing the shops and savoring the chic atmosphere. At the French Market, a rare gourmet provisioner for that era, Carolyn taught me her trick of snatching glistening black coffee beans from the open barrel; once back out on the street, we would grind them up between our teeth and pretend that they were delicious that way. I remember deciding I was in love with her. I don't remember whether I mentioned this to her. In any case, it did not lead to anything sexual. A few years later, for a brief lamentable moment, we did have sex—I'll come to that—but that was after I had worked out that I should repress my desire for boys and get it on with girls.

I also had a simulated going-steady relationship with a girl I met at camp during the summer between ninth and tenth grades. Her name was Susie and she was from the same town in Florida and in the same class at school as my cousin Suzy. On the basis of these coincidences our relationship seemed fated to exist, which indicates its flimsy quality. The only opportunity during the camp day that kids who were coupled off could have any vaguely private time together was in the few minutes after the evening program when everybody was strolling from the Rec Hall to their cabins. Did Susie and I embrace in the gloaming? Surely. Did we kiss? I rather think not. Back home that fall, we exchanged a few letters of the immature and passionless "How are you, I am fine" variety. Also during these years, when I was twelve, thirteen, fourteen and fifteen, I went on occasional dates to parties or movies or dances. But I certainly never had sex with any of those girls. Much less forced myself on them unwanted.

* * *

Eric, a distinguished young scholar of queer history, is arranging to interview me. He's researching a book about the ultra-militant leftist organizations of the sixties, and specifically the participation in them of sexual deviants like me. I use "sexual deviants" here not just because it would have been inelegant to say "queer" twice in two successive sentences, but because at the time people like me were considered by most others to be degenerates, perverts, sickos.

I reckon Eric is about thirty. Like many of his generation he's all over the Internet. To date, we have only spoken briefly on the phone, but I've seen him online. In his videos he is unselfconscious and undefended: cute, sassy, free with the enthusiastic gestures, goofy smiles and eye rolls—as wide-open as the sky about who he is. When I was young such comportment might have got you labeled, with disdain or revulsion, a flamer or a queen, not to mention beaten up. It still could get you beaten up, though the likelihood of that has diminished considerably. And I think this is just how Eric is, naturally, while a flaming queen is often acting a persona, deliberately putting it on. Curiously, the opening page of his website has a different vibe. It's a somber, full-screen, black-and-white photo of him. He's wearing a vaguely military jacket, with arms crossed on his chest. He has an impenetrable gaze, formidable if not quite intimidating. He is square-jawed, handsome and masculine—butch, really, which is to say hypermasculine. Maybe that's the act, Eric's drag of choice, though I haven't yet had enough interaction with him to gauge his sense of humor or penchant for irony. On his site's landing page, aside from the photo and his name, there's just the tagline "Author/Historian/Homosexual." My friend Janet said, "What, 'homosexual' is now a job description?" Maybe not quite, but nowadays it can certainly be a part of somebody's presentation to the world, as proudly embraced and announced as their other accomplishments and distinctions.

In an email Eric said, "I want to focus on your early years as an activist, and how you first grappled with your sexuality." Awfully nosy, I can hear you thinking, from somebody I barely know. But I'm committed to sharing my political experiences with people like him, to help elucidate the radical history of the sixties. And my conviction has long been that the reasons some individuals succumb to the seductions of political violence, as I did, are at least as much psychological as ideological. Which is to say at least partly driven by dark and unconscious urges and needs, sexual impulses and insecurities prominent among them. So it's certainly a question that a historian who wants to portray the period's actors as fully-rounded and flawed human beings should ask.

The years of my activism Eric refers to came later, beginning in 1967 when I was nineteen. I dropped out of college and quickly immersed myself in the radical movement. I became a staff member of Students for a Democratic Society, the largest mass organization on the left in those years. When SDS broke apart in bitter factionalism a few years later, I joined the militant splinter group called the Weathermen, which soon went underground and carried out a campaign of symbolic bombings. My short answer to how, in that combative and testosterone-saturated milieu, I grappled with my sexuality would be, "I butched it up." Which is really just another way to say that I tamped it down. This was not unlike sashaying through the world as a flaming queen—just that the costumes and body moves were different. It meant adopting a persona I felt compelled to portray (that of a *guy*—arty, yes, but a lot of arty cats were balling chicks—to use the quaint and queasy-making period jargon), while hiding that which would give it the lie (my longing to make love with certain boys I loved, and my occasional, usually anonymous, actual, homosexual encounters). The militant persona required some costume changes—chambray work shirts and leather jackets were *de rigeur*—and an angry affect. It also meant learning to mouth a rhetoric of revolution and violence and to actively provoke confrontation. Such camouflage and strutting served even better to hide the lie about my sexual orientation. Or, I must have thought so. I didn't actually think too hard about what I was saying or question what we were doing, much of which I now regret. By butching it up I managed to pass for straight, at least much of the time. Even though butch is hardly how anybody I know, myself included, would describe me. Then or now.

Speaking of drag, I only ever cross-dressed one time in my life, and I did it at Western Junior High School. At the time—I was only twelve or thirteen—I hadn't quite grasped the survival strategy of taking pains not to appear effeminate. I was in eighth grade. I had already experienced plenty of fag-baiting, for my green-and-yellow shirt on Thursdays, for being unathletic, and perhaps for some additional leanings, or fey mannerisms, which were unconscious or out of control. Such as being interested in art and staring at other naked boys in the shower. Maybe the ultimate tipoff would have been, if anybody noticed, the fact that I organized an after-school "Gourmet Club." This consisted of three or four girls I cajoled into joining, and me, and for one or two minutes before he melted away no doubt in embarrassment, my childhood best friend David, the son of Claire and Joe. Having skipped that grade in Taiwan I had left him behind in elementary school when I returned to Washington. But now I was in eighth grade and he was at Western, a year behind me. I recruited one of the Home Economics teachers to be our faculty advisor. (In those days, where I went to school at least, there were classes in Home Ec for girls, held in rooms equipped with sewing machines and complete kitchens, and there were classes in Industrial Arts or "shop"—woodworking, mechanical drawing and such—for boys.)

Just walking into the Home Ec classroom I did feel a twinge of what I would now call transgression of the gender divide. Only I didn't have the concepts of transgression or gender at the time. It just felt vaguely wrong to do, and vulnerable-making, not bold in today's proudly and deliberately queer sense of active transgression. I must have known at some level that this could be ammunition for the mean boys if they had noticed, which they didn't. But

I wasn't doing it as a political act. For me the Gourmet Club was all about glamour and longing—my longing for glamour, I should say. It didn't last more than a few weeks. Two details survive. One was that we learned how to bake chocolate chip cookies, a skill I have actually never used again although I have become quite a good cook. The other was that, with a view to attracting members, I spent my time in art class making posters that featured twinkling nighttime cityscapes—think: soft-focus abstracted views of Manhattan—over which floated the names of world-famous restaurants, or restaurants I assumed were world-famous since I had heard of them, or seen them in movies, although I'd never been to one: Sardi's, 21, Maxim's, La Tour d'Argent. (Can you tell this child would grow up to be homosexual?)

Sometimes after school there was a basketball game. The players were boys, and the cheerleaders were girls. Once each year it was girls on the court and a group of boys leading the cheers, a big school-wide joke. Did I volunteer for this, or did somebody with gaydar—some other repressed homo perhaps, resentfully or sadistically—set me up? There were maybe six of us boys. The real cheerleaders gave us a rudimentary lesson in baton twirling, taught us a routine, and helped us with our costumes, by which I mean the wearing of their uniforms. These consisted of short pleated skirts in green, and white scoop-necked sweaters, the school colors being green and white. For boobs, we each stuffed our sweater with a pair of balloons. At half time, when we strutted out to do our little number, there was general snickering and hilarity from the bleachers. I was giggling too. One of my balloons escaped the sweater and bounced away. That killed, as stand-up comics say. Then it dawned on me that the spectators were not laughing with me, but at me. I don't think I have the coloring to visibly blush, but I suddenly felt hot mortification. And that was the start and finish of my drag career. I can still, however, do the simplest twirl of a baton, or even of a short length of dowel or a stick. This has occasionally proved useful for amusing small children. So the experience wasn't a total loss.

* * *

In the house we lived in before we moved to the Victorian on Drummond Avenue in 1955—the house next door to my little fuck buddy Edmund Laughlin's—on the wall between my parents' bedroom and bathroom there was a panel, framed with molding, maybe three feet high. It was actually there to provide access to the plumbing, and usually hidden by a dresser. One day that piece of furniture was moved, revealing as if by a stroke of magic what to me, at three or four years of age, was certainly a door, lack of hinges and handle notwithstanding. Right away I understood that behind this door was the home of my imaginary friends Walkie and Talkie.

This would have been about 1951 or 1952, when images of World War II and its paraphernalia were still everywhere. "Walkie-talkie" was the colloquial name for an early two-way radio, shaped like a brick but twice as big, developed for use during combat. My friends Walkie and Talkie, who stood about as tall as I, had bodies consisting of these radios plus legs, arms and heads. They were inspired no doubt by cartoony advertising images of the era which similarly anthropomorphized everything from refrigerators to toothpaste tubes to carrots.

My memories of Walkie and Talkie, those humanoid artifacts of innocence, are scant but glowing. They had golden hair. They were apple-cheeked, freckled, and smiley, like the marionette Howdy Doody, then a star of children's TV. They didn't speak, but I heard their thoughts. They could slip right behind that dresser, after it was put back in place, and pass through the little door without it having to open. Life, as this reveals, was wondrous to me. Or, to me the wondrous was unremarkable, and my four-year-old brain assembled its fragments in ways that were perfectly coherent to a four year old. I was also quite sure, for example, that honeysuckle blossoms put in water overnight would make honey, and that the chrome hood ornaments resembling airplanes on certain cars could in fact take flight. I once looked out an upstairs window to see Walkie and Talkie strolling away up the street, holding hands, a sight that gladdened my little heart.

Was that the last time I ever saw them? They didn't move with us to Drummond Avenue because by then I was seven. The world was still kinetic, and kaleidoscopic, but its pieces were beginning to fit together according to a logic I was absorbing from outside myself. I no longer had imaginary friends. I knew that hood ornaments did not fly. And that nobody was invisible.

* * *

We moved to Taipei in 1957, when I was nine. It was at Taipei American School that I was skipped past fifth grade. My grades in fourth were strong. But I suspect this was also a response to my ostensible self-confidence, or audacity. Here's one glimpse: We'd only been in Taipei for a couple of months when Mom wrote this in a chatty letter home: "Last weekend was the performance of Hansel & Gretel in which Marcia danced the part of the mother and, of course, I thought she was very good. Jonny was the gingerbread boy and was on stage for about three or four minutes—but at the curtain call he bowed to the ground just as if he were the star."

That wasn't my first taste of applause. When I was four or five years old, I had a walk-on part in a fashion show put on by Claire and Joe, who had a classy women's clothing store. They were showing what is known as cruise wear. I was dressed in a "cabana set" consisting of a boxer-style bathing suit, in a bright tropical-motif print, and a matching short jacket lined with terry cloth. They didn't sell kids' clothes; I was just there as a sort of prop. Before I went on stage, Claire and Mom both told me I looked gorgeous. The only other people in the show were grown-up women, professional models, but I did not have even a moment's stage fright. The audience, also all women, smiled and cooed.

Here's another look at self-assured me, in Taipei, when I was eleven. Some U.S. dignitary was visiting accompanied by his wife and eleven-year-old daughter. While the bigwig was in his meetings, and the wife was being taken to lunch and shown antique scroll paintings at the museum, or something like that, this girl was delivered to our house so that I could keep her company. I suppose my mother had volunteered me for this quasi-official duty, and I was perfectly happy and not a little proud to take it on. This was long be-fore Taiwan's emergence as a rich economic powerhouse. In her first letter home, Mom had written of "the shock of life as we have never seen it." She described the city as "dusty, mostly dirty, teeming with busy humanity, pedicabs, bicycles, people pushing carts or pulling carts, water buffalos pulling carts, chickens, goats, turkeys, and chil-dren, children and more children. Many [people] live in little tiny shacks or in the back or front of their little stores and businesses and all their family life practically is done in public." But nearly two years on, we were accustomed, or inured, to the conditions, and also enchanted by the city's curiosities and energy. We kids were used to moving around at will without worrying our parents; Taiwan at the time was a police state heavily dependent on the presence of a U.S. military garrison, and nobody in their right mind was going to mess with American Foreign Service brats.

My idea for entertaining my guest that day, which I had ne-glected to mention to anybody else, was to hail a pedicab and take her on a city tour. We visited an ornate Confucian temple I liked, and the lane crammed with antiques stalls called by Americans "Hagglers Row." It was a sticky August day. The pedicab's folding top was up, against the sun, but that didn't interdict the dust and exhaust fumes. So in a flourish of what I supposed to be gracious hosting I took her finally to the calmest and fanciest place in town, the Grand Hotel. We sat on a terrace above the city; waiters brought us crullers and iced tea. Pedicab travel through Taipei's bustling streets was slow. We turned up back home late in the day to find both of our mothers in a state of tightly controlled panic—hers in fear for her probably, mine perhaps more in fear of a faux pas. It hadn't occurred to me to consider that anybody might be alarmed at my taking this girl who knows where. I was bold in doing so, and the possibility of risk didn't occur to me. The girl herself was tight-lipped the whole afternoon, probably controlling her own anxiety.

Now, back in Chevy Chase, the cohort I'd been part of since kindergarten was still in sixth grade at the cozy elementary school a block from our Drummond Avenue house. But I was in seventh, at the junior high school, where my classmates were strangers who all seemed to know each other and were older than me. I was an eleven-year-old child in a student population that ranged in age up to fifteen. My family hadn't arrived back in Washington until early November, eight weeks into the school year. If you ever survived the torture of junior high school, you will recognize my mortification at being introduced—on a single day, in front of six different classrooms full of strangers—as The New Kid. Cue the sniggers, and prepare for the bullying. I was confused and scared.

Even though the bullying I experienced was mainly nasty jokes and menacing glares, I was physically scared. I was scared of, and fascinated by, other boys' bodies. I wanted to touch them and could easily imagine them attacking me if they somehow noticed. I was bewildered at the time by my own body. Puberty had not skipped ahead a year when I did; I was still a little boy, physically. Also, sports had never interested me in the least. In Taipei, Mom had sent me for lessons with the tennis pro at the Grand Hotel; after two sessions he declared me hopeless and refused to try with me again. Now there was the daily ordeal of gym class and competitive athletics, with their requirements and rituals. I had never heard of a jock strap. What was it for? Where could you buy one? How did you even put it on? But I was instructed to get one right away to complete my gym suit. Gym suit?

* * *

Kathy and Mike Birnbaum and their four kids arrived in Taipei a few months after we did. Mike, a Brooklyn Jew, had sensibilities my parents instantly grokked and a sense of humor they loved. Kathy, English and a shiksa—a non-Jew—was smart, playful, great company, and an equal-opportunity flirt. The two families hit it off right away. Some of us kids were aligned in age and became pals. My future step-brother David and I sometimes rode our bikes to a chaotic street market, or out to the airport to loop the runway—it was a sleepy airport, with few daily flights—and to play inside the unlocked cockpits of parked planes. Often, we all went to a magnificent ocean beach which took on a different wind-sculpted dune topography week by week. It was always nearly empty because it was a military reservation and off-limits to all but the diplomatic corps. Abe and Mike would pound bamboo poles into the sand, to support a big candy-striped shade canopy. In my mother's letters, glowing mentions of Kathy were frequent. Surprisingly soon after they met, Mom wrote to her girlfriends at home, "When you have a friend you can let your hair down with over a cup of coffee, it's divine, need I tell you?"

The Grand Hotel held film screenings on Sunday nights. Mom mentions in a letter that the movies were always a year or two out of date and the projector usually broke down halfway through. On one particular Sunday, Mike was away somewhere, and Kathy was over for supper. Why I was the only kid home I cannot explain. After dinner, the three grownups talked about whether to go over to the Grand. This was in late 1958 or early 1959. Let's imagine that evening's offering was the 1957 romance *An Affair to Remember* with Cary Grant and Deborah Kerr. As it happened, my parents had seen the film, whatever it was, but Kathy had not. Mom declared that she didn't want to see it again. My father promptly volunteered to take Kathy. And within minutes, as I recollect the scene, those two swept out of the house and drove off.

Our house had a thirty-five-foot living room. It was open all along one side to a glassed-in porch. Centered on the opposite long wall was a fireplace. We used that on cool winter evenings; in subtropical Taiwan, central heating was little known. There was a dining table at one end of the big room, and a sofa and lounge chairs grouped by the fireplace, and other chairs and tables on the porch. Many times, all six of us had comfortably inhabited this expansive room at once, each absorbed in some separate pursuit. It had easily accommodated dinner parties and cocktail parties, and once a Hanukah party for, as Mom described it in a letter, "some forty-odd—and I do mean odd—Jews."

After my father and his future second wife left for the movie, Mom sat alone in the big living room, sobbing.

The only light was from a single lamp. She looked very small in this spacious dark interior.

I went into the bedroom wing. I came back to the living room. She was still sobbing.

I stood next to her chair. I put my hand on her shoulder. She sobbed. Neither of us spoke a word. I went to my room again.

I have not invented this scene, though I may have embellished the memory. But there was corroboration that something was going on. Not long afterward, I was playing with Ashley and David Birnbaum who are respectively a year older and a year younger than me. Juvenile chatter, relating without comprehending things overheard: "When our father came back, he had a big fight with our mother. They were in the shower together but we still heard. He said he didn't want her to see your father any more." Oh. Okay.

* * *

Foreign Service postings were typically for two years. Then you were given a couple of months for home leave. After that, normally, you resumed your post for a second tour of duty. My brothers and I had been having a blast in Taipei. My father loved his work there, and would have been happy to return for that second stint. Mom enjoyed it, too. I know this for sure, because I have that scrapbook of letters she wrote to her friends at home. But my sister Marcia, who is six years older than me, had been studying modern dance since she was little. She was so determined to make a career as a dancer that she had convinced my parents to send her back to Washington after our first year in Taiwan, alone, when she was sixteen, so that she could resume her training. She lived that year with a family friend while she was in eleventh grade at Bethesda-Chevy Chase High School, taking a bus and then a streetcar back and forth into the city nearly every afternoon, to the Georgetown dance studio of her teachers Evelyn de la Tour and Pola Nirenska.

(Is it any surprise that Marcia was at home in Georgetown, with her exotically European *artiste* mentors Eve and Pola, her unusual experience of international travel and cultures, and her determination to be an artist herself? She was an inspiration to me in my adolescent years when I imagined myself doing something, anything, in the arts. The sophistication she manifested appealed to me. Significantly, I ignored the more vital role-modeling she provided, of such essential qualities for success in the arts, or in anything, as focus and perseverance.)

I must have thought I was to be in school at Western Junior High just for our few weeks of home leave. Then we would return to dazzlingly exotic Taiwan and our delicious life there. I loved living in Taipei and was eager to go back. But Marcia was in her senior year. She would be making big decisions about college and her future. Mom was troubled by the idea of not being present to support her.

At the front of every classroom at Western, above the blackboard, there was a clock. Since it was electric, even if you got up on a ladder and put your ear against it you wouldn't have heard any sinister ticking. Still, it marked a countdown. If you were bored, or getting a headache from the binomial theorem, you watched that clock for its promise of release. If you were anxious about completing an assignment, you might avoid looking at it, or else not be able to stop yourself doing so. Usually what was coming was simply the bell, signaling the end of the period and setting free two thousand kids to bang through the halls toward their next classes. Then there was one afternoon when, to me alone, the sweep of its second hand suggested not ticking but hissing, a slow leak toward deflation and collapse: the departure time of a certain flight from Washington National on which my family and I would not, after all, be traveling. The tickets had been issued—paper ones, they were back then. I had held them in my hands.

From where I sat, Taipei looked increasingly distant and golden. I had felt safe there. Without understanding much about why they came my way, I enjoyed all kinds of treats and privileges from being in a Foreign Service family. I loved the impossibly green mountains, terraced with rice paddies, that you could see from the city. And the lively markets, and the tranquil walled gardens surrounding the houses people like us lived in. Now in Washington it was November and getting darker. I was lonely. School was threatening. I watched the classroom clock leak out the minutes while at the airport that plane boarded and its passengers settled into their seats. As if being on that flight, and going back to Taipei, could have whisked me back to the sunny place of childhood and innocence. Which is to say, to that time before oncoming puberty, when I was still untroubled by sex.

Those tickets went unused. We stayed where we were. Only my childhood flew away.

* * *

The other day, I was telling my friend Paula about our not returning to Taiwan, which has always seemed so consequential to me. I trotted out the established explanation: Mom couldn't bear the idea of being away while Marcia completed high school and prepared for college.

"Sure," said Paula, a mother herself. "But what about your father? Didn't it undermine his career?" Actually, I don't think it interfered with Daddy's career. If it did, then not much and not for long.

"And your mother?" asked Paula. "What else was going on, for her?"

I know that my mother missed her parents, and especially missed her close women friends in Washington. That would have given her additional motivation.

I also know that Mom knew, or at least suspected, that my father had fallen for Kathy.

Boing.

I knew this to be true at the age of eleven though I didn't have the words, or even the concept. But I knew *something*. I had seen Mom's reaction when Abe and Kathy left for the movie. I was the only one who saw it. I did not tell anyone else, not for years to come. And until now, when Paula asked, I had never considered that Mom's knowledge of something going on between her husband and her friend might have increased her reluctance to return for a second tour, which would have placed those two in the same city on the other side of the globe once again.

I was just paging again through my mother's letters from Taipei. Despite having read them dozens of times before, somehow

I never registered this passage, which is another indication of the unreliable, or selective, nature of memory. My memory. Mom wrote, "There is really nothing new in our lives except that we are on the last lap now and in six months or so, we will be saying goodbye to Taiwan and I am already quite nostalgic and sentimental about doing so . . . I am now looking at everything with renewed interest because I want to remember how everything here looks. As I perhaps have already mentioned to you, Abe would really love to come back for another tour—but because of Marcia and also my learning of my father's recent illness—I have influenced him otherwise."

So we never were to go back. The tickets never had been issued. I never had held them in my hands. My vivid memory of clock-watching misery in that classroom at Western Junior High is a fabrication.

But my misery there in seventh grade was not.

* * *

On occasional Saturdays when I was in seventh grade, during the winter before I had that jolting encounter with Cousin Leonard's casual racism, I also "worked" for my father's brother Leon. Uncle Leon had a hardware store on Seventh Street, NW, in Washington's Black ghetto. The store was narrow, dark, dusty, and depressing. For our lunch he would heat up a can of beans, on a single-burner hot plate under a hanging, bare light bulb, in the clutter of a windowless back room. Leon was depressing, too, overweight, angry, and cheerless. He was probably clinically depressed. He was probably not getting any help for it.

I didn't know anything about hardware so can't have been much help in the store. But I did quickly learn to wait on the broken-down men who stumbled in and headed to where the paints and solvents were shelved. They asked for "denatured." That was denatured alcohol. These did not seem to be guys who had run short of thinner in the middle of paint jobs; they could hardly stand up. Denatured alcohol, I did not know at the time, is the pure stuff amended with chemicals that make it variously foul-smelling, nauseating or downright poisonous, so as to discourage its recreational consumption. In its favor, it was cheap. A pint sold for twenty-five cents. By number of purchases if not earnings, it was the store's top seller. This was confusing.

Leon's store was burned out during the massive riot triggered by the 1968 murder of Martin Luther King Jr. He committed suicide shortly after that. That was not so confusing—or, by then I was twenty and adult enough to hazard a few guesses why: his likely sense of financial failure, especially compared to my father and their younger brother Joe, both of whom had advanced degrees and stable professional careers that would provide comfortable retirements; his tempestuous marriage and family life; his obesity and the surgery he had just had to remove part of his digestive tract; the daunting challenge, at fifty-something, of starting over at the burned-out store or finding another way to make a living. I also have long suspected that he may have called it quits with life because he was gay and closeted. Take this theory with caution, though; people who know me well say I'm forever wishfully detecting homosexuality where it just as likely doesn't exist. And none of my siblings ever thought that about Leon, although there is family lore that he had been troubled, perhaps bullied, in high school, which might at least circumstantially support my theory. I would like to ask Leon some questions, and about more than his sexuality. Like, what did he think about selling alcoholics a known poison, at an easily afforded twenty-five cents a bottle? How did he feel about relations between Blacks and whites? Was he saddened or angered by King's murder, or perhaps even gratified? Was he surprised at the uprising it provoked? Did it occur to him that he fitted a resented pattern of Jews owning businesses in Black communities? Did he perhaps blame the loss of his store on antisemitism, and see himself as a victim? I'll never know.

* * *

In my miserable first years of junior high, I was waylaid by periodic unpredictable swellings. I could wake up, for instance, with my upper lip bulging grotesquely. My brother Steve, who is now possibly

the gentlest man alive but at the time enjoyed picking on his siblings, called these "pig lips," and was glad to announce—using a
nickname he had bestowed which I also didn't care for—"Look,
Snerdie has a pig lip." At other times one eye might be swollen
nearly shut. Swelling could afflict my tongue, or my throat, or the
heel or ball of a foot forcing me to limp. Some of these episodes,
which might last a day or more, especially the visible ones, made
good excuses to stay home from school. Most likely that's why my
body was producing them. They were diagnosed as angioneurotic
edema, which can have many etiologies including anxiety and
stress. I felt somewhat comforted by the "neurotic" part, which
seemed sophisticated and worldly and to deflect the focus from
my body to my psyche. But I didn't like the experiences.

My mother began to realize that I dreaded school. She tried
gently to get me to say why. Now I think she knew, but we never
named it. I did not say I was being bullied. I didn't think of what
I experienced as bullying. And I did not at the time have conversations about myself and homosexuality with Mom or anybody
else. People didn't name it much then, except disparagingly or as
an expletive, and then they mostly used one of its other names,
the ones the boys at school lobbed at me, like faggot or queer. In
those days, in the culture at large, gay still meant cheerful and
charming. My father occasionally used the locution "that way,"
delivered with a put-on, mincing smirk and eye roll as in, "Oh,
is he *that way?*" But he was also clueless. My step-mother related
that once, when they took their seats for the first dinner on an
ocean-liner crossing of the Atlantic, there was another couple at
their table for six, plus two men. "Well," my father asked, quite
guilelessly I'm sure, "and where are *your* womenfolk?" And here's
a joke of Abe's, reliant on multiple stereotypes and always delivered in a Yiddish accent: Mrs. Cohen runs into Mrs. Goldberg.
"Did you hear," she asks, "The Feinstein boy is a homosexual!"
Mrs. Goldberg replies, "Vey iz mir! That's terrible!" Mrs. Cohen
says, "Yes, but he's going with a nice Jewish wrestler."

Abe was a product of his time, as are we all. And there were
a lot of words people had trouble calmly uttering then, such as

slavery, or cancer, or impending death. I finally steeled myself to look up "homosexuality" in the encyclopedia. I skimmed a few sentences describing what appeared to be a disease as tragic as leprosy, and slammed the big book shut in panic.

Mom suggested several possibilities: I could see a psychiatrist. No! I'm not *really* neurotic! I could go to a boarding school in England called Summerhill. Summerhill was a miniature experiment in ultra-democracy; the kids had equal votes to the faculty's, curricula were self-determined and classes optional. In theory that intrigued me, but the idea of going someplace so distant and different, alone, was frightening. I had already once suffered through being the new kid at school who knew nobody and whom nobody knew. By the time I was out of junior high I was feeling more self-confident, and less threatened. Puberty had arrived, and I had made some friends. I'm not sure which of these two factors was more instrumental in dissipating my gloom but I wouldn't discount the importance of the former—beginning to grow into my adult body seemed to make me both more invisible and more acceptable, because it rendered me more masculine.

By high school I was at another enormous suburban education factory, which I didn't love. I probably claimed to hate it, but affected alienation was a fashionable attitude among the arty, leftish kids I hung out with—by then I did have friends, whom I enjoyed. So I can't remember exactly what precipitated my transfer, with Mom's support, to Hawthorne, for eleventh grade. Like, why then? I want to think that she intuited my conflicted sexuality, and also understood—even if nobody had ever told her in words—that she didn't have long to live. If those things are true, then I can imagine that she wanted to make me as comfortable as possible while she could.

In my first year at Hawthorne, the school occupied a decrepit if once-grand city-center town house. It was like something enchanted from a bedtime story. At the start of my senior year, the school moved into a newly constructed building that fed a different sort of fantasy. It was located in a formerly impoverished Black neighborhood that had been bulldozed for redevelopment. This was a backstory I was dimly aware of, but scarcely considered. Very little had been built so far on the area's now-blank acres other than our school, a couple of contemporary-style apartment buildings in one direction and a new playhouse for the Arena Stage theater in another. There was a somewhat lunar emptiness, but this vastness scattered with modernist structures, like brave pioneers, seemed to be further evidence of mid-century promise.

Compared to the makeshift wreck of a school building we were leaving behind Hawthorne's new home had an utterly different spirit, of rationality and openness. Its design well reflected the school's culture. In addition to standard classrooms, for example, there was a many-windowed corner room dedicated to a social studies course called Senior Seminar, where twelfth graders met for three hour sessions twice a week. At the school's heart was a double-height atrium with one glass wall and an upstairs gallery on the other three sides, from which regular classrooms were entered. The whole school came together there for a meeting every mid-morning, with the landing of a free-standing staircase serving as podium. Some may have found the new building's brutalist style and unfinished concrete surfaces cold. I loved it because it was modern and bold. It also echoed my family's move from the shingle-style Drummond Avenue Victorian, with its leaded-glass windows, secret passages, and big front porch, into our austere International Style house, which itself had a two-story living room surrounded by a second-floor gallery. Neither the new school nor our new house gave off the slightest suggestion of childhood and fairy tales. These tasteful, grown-up buildings seemed like anterooms to my future.

* * *

I had known Violet and various other maids, and Daisy in my second grade class, and those Negro TV characters, and Mr. Hatton the chauffeur. I had been acquainted with them, more accurately. But I didn't think about Black people politically, which is to say about racism, until the civil rights movement entered my consciousness. Then, in the same naive and nuance-obliterating way that I assumed all my family's friends and relatives were in favor of racial integration, I considered everything about Maryland, my home state, to be liberal and freedom-loving. And I thought that everything about Virginia, across the Potomac River to the south, was racist and a little scary.

Certain facts seemed to support this oversimplification. Daisy, that lone Black girl, integrated my Maryland classroom in 1955, just a year after Brown v Board of Education. Virginia's reaction to that Supreme Court ruling was "massive resistance," and its state and local governments fought integration well into the seventies. I was also smugly proud that Maryland did not secede and join the Confederacy during the Civil War—not that anyone in my family had lived in Maryland, or even on this continent, until a half century later. But I overlooked the inconvenient detail that Maryland was actually a slave state. Virginia, in further support of my superficial grasp of things, had been home not only to the Confederacy's capital, Richmond, but also to its sainted military leader Robert E. Lee. Besides, I had witnessed, from the car window, what I always thought of as chain gangs working on the roads of Virginia. But I checked the history just now. Those must have been mere convict labor details, the convicts not chained together, though they were overseen by armed guards. The use of actual chain gangs had been discontinued before I was born. But still.

Whenever out-of-town relatives or friends visited, we would take them sightseeing to places like the Washington Monument, and Mount Vernon where Martha and George Washington had lived. Another of those American holy places we would take our visitors to see was the Lincoln Memorial. From there, Memorial Bridge crosses the Potomac directly on axis with Arlington House, a temple-form Greek Revival mansion once the home of Robert E. Lee. The house remained a shrine of sorts to him. It sits on a commanding rise in the middle of Arlington National Cemetery; the cemetery acreage itself had been Lee's plantation. Memorial Bridge, elegant with repeating low stone arches, crosses the water from one zone of monuments to another, a ceremonial boulevard. Coupling

Lee to Lincoln like this, in an equivalence of nobility, it is an artifact of the revisionist American history of race.

There is a different bridge over the Potomac, called Chain Bridge, closer to where we lived when I was a kid, which we took perhaps more often to get to Virginia. I crossed it several times riding along with my mother, when she went to visit a woman called Irma. That's a name without glitter, and as out of date now as Elsie. Irma had also undergone a mastectomy or two, and then established a cottage industry making breast prostheses with which to fill out other women's empty brassieres. Naturally, my mother and I never discussed Irma's handicrafts or Mom's need for them. These visits to Irma must have been before we went to Taipei, because I recall that I would be sent outside to play, as a little kid would be. The chain link fence at the rear of Irma's backyard was heavy with honeysuckle. I idly swung sticks at the bees hovering around it, and generally ambled around bored, with no other kids in the picture. I assumed then that the two women only sat at the kitchen table chatting and drinking coffee. But they must have been doing something more technical, involving measuring and fitting the replacement breasts. A few years later, when we had returned from Taipei to Washington, I overheard Mom say to Daddy, sotto voce, simply, "Irma died." If they talked about that further, it would have been out of my earshot, but if they didn't it would have been consistent with our family habit of silence.

I crossed Chain Bridge soon after Mom died when I drove myself, on impulse and unannounced, to visit Kathy, her friend whom my father would marry. I remember sitting with Kathy in her living room—a glassy space with a view into trees—both of us mute. Whatever I hoped she would say to me I can't recall, if I even knew at the time. I also couldn't know then that she and I would eventually become great and lasting friends.

Chain Bridge lacks the grandeur and scale of Memorial Bridge. Although as a child I erroneously assumed its name had something to do with chain gangs, it is called Chain Bridge because its early nineteenth-century precursor was a suspension bridge depended from iron chains. The one there now, the same one I knew as a kid, in contrast to Memorial Bridge, is a narrow and graceless span. It is the bridge I crossed with such exuberance, driving my classmates in the blue Studebaker to Charlottesville and Bremo. And before I was old enough to drive, it is the bridge I crossed on the way to Irma's with my mother at the wheel, our conversation desultory. That recollection is veiled in sorrow.

3

Cool Kids

For a little while when I was in junior high, my prize possession was a General Electric clock radio. In that era when the appliances, like the cars, were ridiculously tricked up with fins and swoops and shiny surfaces to look "modernistic" or "space-age," my radio was atypically simple, a rectangle larger than a brick but smaller than a cinder block, in baby-blue plastic. It was minimalist by default since it was the cheapest model, I think I bought it for $11. Its only illumination was a feeble glow from the vacuum tubes inside. In bed, in my room on the third floor of the Drummond Avenue Victorian, with its under-the-eaves slanted ceiling, with the lights off and the radio giving out its faint hum, I felt protected from the taunts and humiliations of the school day. And I felt aspirationally grown up, because I listened on that radio to Steve Allison. He was an early practitioner of talk radio, who broadcast live in the evenings from a steak house downtown. My older brother and his pals sometimes went there to witness the performances in person, which seemed an enviably adultish sort of activity I might replicate when I was old enough. Steve Allison was mildly provocative and often—deliciously—rude to his callers. He told jokes that ranged from delightfully corny to scandalously outrageous.

Here's one I was embarrassed to have snickered at even at the time and in the solitude of my bedroom.

To get the joke, you need to recall that during those years around 1960, African colonies were being jettisoned by their European overlords. Even someone as marginally conscious of international news as I was at the time would have been aware that these newly liberated countries could be unstable, wracked by rivalries and civil wars (and as we now know, by the machinations of their European former rulers and interference from U.S. government agencies including the one my father worked for). The exotic-sounding names of their political leaders would have been familiar enough from the news, too, even if their various factions and the politics they espoused were confusing. Kwame Nkrumah of Ghana. Félix Houphouët-Boigny of Ivory Coast. In the especially conflicted former Belgian colony Congo there were Moïse Tshombe, Joseph-Désiré Mobutu, Joseph Kasa-Vubu, and Patrice Lumumba who was assassinated after—pardon this historical oversimplification—falling out with other three. So, Steve Allison's on-air joke:

Kasa-Vubu is having lunch with Mobutu. "You like Lumumba?" he asks? "Go ahead! Have some more!"

I was shocked at the suggestion of cannibalism, but titillated by the linguistic trick involved, and then ashamed that my reaction was racist, and glad nobody had heard me snicker.

* * *

My ninth grade English teacher at Western Junior High School was Bruce Lewis. Everybody should get at least one teacher like him who makes you work hard and love what you're learning. Everybody probably doesn't. Mr. Lewis could be very funny. His discourse was oblique and thrillingly sardonic, hinting at an occult grownup language we were vouchsafed to overhear and might someday learn to speak. He could be almost frighteningly intense. He demanded precision, and in the end you valued the work he exacted. It's possible that he was a model of collegiality, but I got the feeling he didn't have much time for the rest of the faculty, because he seemed to live larger, less drably. Or maybe it was I who didn't have time for the faculty, other than for him. That year I was in ninth grade he drove a red MGB roadster. Later he replaced it with a red Thunderbird convertible. These were sexy cars. He wore chinos, and tweed jackets and Weejun loafers. The school was full to bursting with baby-boom students and had run out of space. Aptly, his classes were held down the hill in the meeting room of the branch library. We were privileged to leave the building to get there, but we had to get there on time or suffer his mordant gaze. To have Mr. Lewis for English was an ambiguous distinction. The kids who didn't were thankful. But many of us who did were thankful too, smugly so.

For a year or two after we had moved on to high school, a group from my year continued to meet with him in an informal literary club. Now it was awkward! Should we call him Mr. Lewis, or could we call him Bruce? We resolved the problem by referring to him among ourselves simply as Lewis, and by not directly addressing him by name. Boundaries had been blurred without being illuminated; he wasn't exactly our teacher any more but we weren't his equals, and he wasn't exactly our friend either. We all assumed that he was a homo, although I don't remember anybody being especially freaked out by that. And maybe his singularity had some other explanation. He did speak with a drawl, a frequent caricature of fags back then, but that was easily put down to his being Southern. And plenty of people in Maryland had Southern accents. Actually, if I ever knew where he came from, or anything about his family or personal life, I've forgotten. His astringency verged on what I referred to earlier as the bitter acid of drag humor—though I couldn't have made that association then because at the time I had no awareness of drag. But he was altogether too cool and iconoclastic to be normal; if he was homosexual, it would hardly have been his most noteworthy quality.

I have wondered why he bothered teaching in a junior high school. This is shameful of me, since I so appreciate having had him for a teacher when I was thirteen, and teaching kids to think is a mighty high calling. Still, if he'd wanted, he had the brilliance to do something better remunerated and better regarded. Maybe he didn't need the money. Maybe he didn't need the regard, either. He already had a rather lofty opinion of himself. Maybe he liked the short work day and long vacations, because he actually had something else to do. Maybe he was writing the Great American Novel. Or—it's not impossible—maybe teaching school was worth it to him because it gave him some space, so that he could risk conducting a secret life. For all any of us knew he spent his summers romping in a skimpy bathing suit on the beach at Provincetown or Fire Island. Secrecy would have been an existential necessity for a homosexual public school teacher back then.

Our literary club meetings took place on Sunday afternoons, rotating between our houses. Mr. Lewis often showed up accompanied by a friend who was only ever known to us as O'Reilly. O'Reilly may too have been smart as a whip, I can't recall. But he was flabby and indifferently dressed; he lacked Mr. Lewis's dash. We speculated that they could be boyfriends, although it was hard to see the appeal of O'Reilly. So there was this murmur among us about one or both of them being queer. The girls perhaps felt safer for it. I don't think the boys minded, or felt threatened, or were threatened in fact. For me, murkily conflicted though I was about my own sexuality, Bruce Lewis probably radiated a glimmer of possibility. Not the possibility that I might have sex with him myself. I'm sure I never brought myself to imagine that, if for no other reason than I couldn't yet actually picture men having sex. But he represented the possibility that a man could be homosexual—if he was—and brilliant, and occupy a respected place in the world. And drive a sexy car. I was crestfallen though when my friend Sue laughingly repeated something she'd overheard her mother say to another mother on the phone. "It's fine with me if Sue wants to be part of it. But if it were my son, boy, then I'd worry." Even somebody like Sue, my friend, laughing, thought there was something at least ridiculous about homosexuals. At the time, I mean. I'm sure she no longer does.

Of course at the time so did I.

When the literary club met at my house, we would sit around in the den. What were we reading? Carson McCullers maybe, or Katherine Anne Porter? Joseph Conrad? I have a memory of Mom stepping into the room one time, to say hello to Mr. Lewis and the group. I realize now that for a long time I have collapsed that memory with one from a different time when she came into the den where I was sitting alone with a book. I know it was a different time, in a way that makes me squirm, because this second event was only weeks before she died, and as I said, I had already been told that her cancer was terminal. And I know this was not the time she said hello to the group because she died when I was in twelfth grade, when the literary club had long since stopped meeting. The book I was holding, this second time that makes me squirm to remember, was James Agee's *A Death in the Family*. I wasn't actually reading it. I couldn't bring myself to read it. But its title had irresistibly compelled me to take it off a shelf at the library and bring it home. My mother took it in with a glance. And as we were so well accustomed to not doing, neither of us uttered a word.

I wrote that yesterday, which happened to be December 14, the date of her death in 1964. My older brother Steve believes firmly that people's moods are influenced by personally significant anniversaries. He's a clinical psychologist and has studied the phenomenon. Or at least observed it in himself: Most years, he emails or calls on that date, wanting to share his feeling of sadness, and tell me he loves me. This anniversary reaction generally doesn't operate in me. My memorial clock only rang in that way, and loudly enough, when I had reached exactly the age at which Mom died, thirty-three years after the fact, when my own psychotherapist suggested that my depression was a function of not yet having grieved for her. I have most years not even remembered the date's significance until it's passed or I am reminded by one of my siblings. I was aware this time that it was the anniversary, because I am busy now with this remembrance, which keeps turning on the pivotal fact of her death. Steve didn't call yesterday, either, for a change.

* * *

I've been poring over online maps of Washington's Maryland suburbs. The names of streets and neighborhoods that I once knew so well, and their glimpses on Street View, are evocative. For example, an image of one particular driveway on East Halbert Road in the subdivision called Bannockburn conjured up a bunch of friends milling around and sitting on the curb there one evening in the summer of our high school graduation, not knowing what to say, after we'd heard that our friend Brooke had crashed his motorcycle and died.

A lot of the kids I first got to know in junior high school, including some who were in the literary club, lived in Bannockburn, which is a few miles further from D.C. than where we lived, and in Bethesda not Chevy Chase. Bannockburn was established in the forties as a sort of cooperative community by couples with young families and optimistic leftish ideas. The houses were modest, but modernist, efficiently designed and thoughtfully sited along the hilly streets. There were only a couple of models, but they were placed differently on their lots to fit the terrain, and tweaked to avoid a cookie-cutter streetscape. One design could even be completely reversed, having a plausible main entryway on both its front and back facades. And the houses were differentiated by varying rooflines and permutating treatments of brick and wood siding. Thus a hopeful balance was established between individuality and uniformity, achievement of which must have been an unsettling if subconscious preoccupation for many people in that post-war, cold-war, witch-hunt era, especially for people who might have been described as, or accused of, being leftists.

I've always had an eye for architecture. I spent endless afternoons as a kid drawing floor plans. I used to love climbing through the partly constructed houses that were filling in then around where we lived. Most of my magazine-writing career has been concerned with topics like architecture and urban planning, too. Bannockburn was an inspiration, for its design sensibility, and also for its less tangible qualities of community. It gave me a glimmer of understanding that those things can be connected.

So today I was wandering around Bannockburn on Street View, and then started tracing various routes from there to where I lived. One route goes past another, later, modernist subdivision called Potomac Overlook. These houses are perched on a thickly wooded bluff just above the river. They're bigger and more luxurious than the rather no-frills Bannockburn designs, and the wooded terrain they are set in is even steeper. But a similar aesthetic undergirds both neighborhoods. Through the thick foliage, on my monitor, I couldn't identify the particular one of these houses that I toured with Mom when it was newly built and on the market. In my possibly burnished recollection, it was snugged into the slope, with its several descending levels all opening into a soaring, multistory screened porch. I lusted after it. Mom liked it too, but we couldn't have afforded it. At the time, we were still living on Drummond Avenue, in the house with the window seats and nooks and crannies. Wonderful that place was, but it wasn't modern, which is what I felt myself to be, and how I wanted to be seen.

The houses in Potomac Overlook, including that one I lusted after, were designed by an architecture firm which is renowned for the quantity and quality of modernism it has bequeathed to the Washington area. One of that firm's principals was Donald Lethbridge. Curiously, he and his family also lived in a quirky old house much like ours and just two doors down on Drummond Avenue; Mr. Lethbridge was a modernist but also a historic preservationist. When we moved a few blocks away to that distinctive International Style house, Mr. Lethbridge, modernist and preservationist both, was eager to come see it. One of its unusual features was that all the windows were tall casements opening inward. We were planning to build a deck at the rear off the living room. Lethbridge was politely horrified that our idea was to tear open the wall and install of-the-moment sliding glass doors. He suggested that we just turn one set of casements into French doors instead. What was obvious to him hinted at a lesson for me about preservation architecture: First, do no harm.

One of Lethbridge's earliest projects was a post-war subdivision across the river in Falls Church, Virginia, called Holmes Run

Acres. Its houses were like Bannockburn's in scale and contemporary style. And their DNA was alive and recognizable in his later, more glamorous work at Potomac Overlook. Here's another chain bridge: Holmes Run Acres is where my future step-mother Kathy lived with her first husband and their four kids, before Taiwan, before we ever knew them.

* * *

Spending all this time looking at digital maps of where I grew up, it occurred to me that I've never known exactly where the line runs between Chevy Chase and Bethesda. Then I made a discovery—a pair of discoveries—which should not be unsettling, but strangely are.

According to Wikipedia, "an unincorporated community, Bethesda has no official boundaries. The United States Census Bureau defines a census-designated place [CDP] named Bethesda . . . Other definitions are used by the Bethesda Urban Planning District, the United States Postal Service . . . and other organizations."

And Wikipedia says, "Chevy Chase is the name of both a town and an unincorporated census-designated place." It enumerates several incorporated villages distinct from the Town of Chevy Chase that include Chevy Chase in their names, such as North Chevy Chase. "The United States Postal Service uses Chevy Chase for some postal addresses that lie outside historical Chevy Chase." Thus it is the postal service's less bounded idea of Chevy Chase that includes the tiny, one-street, incorporated Village of Drummond, where my family lived. It also includes the adjacent neighborhood called Somerset, where we later lived in the Bauhaus-derived architectural gem with the two-story living room. Somerset too is an incorporated town. I had always assumed that Drummond, which currently has forty-three households, and Somerset, which has four hundred seven, were both situated within and constituent parts of the Town of Chevy Chase, but I was wrong. They are separate geopolitical entities. "These villages, the town, and the CDP share a common history and together form a larger community colloquially referred to as Chevy Chase."

So despite a reliable sense of direction and sharp visual memories of where I lived until I left for college at seventeen, I have stumbled on the fact that I never was a resident of Chevy Chase, Maryland. Municipally speaking, that is. I grew up there, or in a place called that. But it seems I was a resident of Chevy Chase only "colloquially." This probably shouldn't be unnerving, but it makes me feel wobbly and ungrounded. At least I did reside during childhood in a legally defined local place, or two: the Village of Drummond and then the Town of Somerset.

As for my friends in Bannockburn, they lived in Bethesda— or "Bethesda"—but only notionally, because that name exists not to identify a town but simply to serve the needs of mail carriers and census enumerators, and I suppose realtors. Of course, citizenship is conferred by the nation, not by one's most local municipality. And we all did grow up within defined entities, one within the next: Montgomery County, the State of Maryland, the U.S.A., and Planet Earth. Still, I feel somehow undermined, as if I can feel one more fact of my youth slipping away and not, for a change, because my memory is failing me.

Montgomery County has five hundred seven square miles, the vast majority of which when I was a kid were rural and culturally Southern, that is conservative, not suburban and more liberal like Bethesda or Chevy Chase. If casually asked now where I hail from, I never respond "Maryland" or "Montgomery County," or for that matter cite as my "home town" the laughably anachronistic Village of Drummond nor similarly quaint Somerset, both being entirely residential and thus hard to credit as real places for growing up: neither ever had a barber shop, burger joint, movie theater, gas station or anything but houses plus, in Somerset, the elementary school and a community pool. Of course, it depends who's asking, and when. If, during my high school years, somebody from elsewhere in "Bethesda" or "Chevy Chase" wondered where exactly I lived I would have said Somerset. When somebody now asks where I'm from my first reply is to say Washington, where I am not "from" in the sense of actually having lived in the District of Columbia while I was growing up. But I suppose a sense of dislocation, geographic or otherwise, is something I share in a loose and inverted way with quite a few other Americans today—since so many are so exercised about issues of origins (other peoples', mostly) and of belonging (and who may not).

* * *

As a young child, I wasn't much concerned with being judged or measuring up. In adolescence, that changed. This was not just because the omnipresent message got through to me that the physical contact I wanted, with boys, was wrong and must be hidden. Nor was it just because of the miseries of junior high. Suddenly adulthood was visible in the near distance, inexorably approaching. Cobbling together a viable persona for grown-up life seemed urgent, even if it required imposture.

Not knowing much never kept me from pretending to know more. Not understanding a text or lyric didn't stop me memorizing and reciting it. Not having read a book or seen a movie didn't discourage me from allowing as how I had done so already—especially a book or movie exalted by or even simply mentioned by anybody whose approval I hoped for. I resorted to these pretensions so as not to appear unenlightened or green. This was despite the fact that like every teenaged reader of my time and class, I emulated Holden Caulfield whose signal characteristic was his contempt for phonies. Oh well. I stopped feeling bad about this type of dishonesty a long time ago. I was eager to be grown up, and a personality under construction is a spacious and flexible edifice, easily accommodating contradiction. Mr. Lewis' tutelage in critical thinking and precise expression didn't include guidance on self-awareness, or modesty. He tried to instill intellectual integrity, but other strong influences, including a lack of confidence and the desire to hide it, encouraged something else.

Starting when I was eleven, when we got back from Taiwan, I attended Hebrew school, principally to prepare for my bar mitzvah. My family was more culturally than religiously Jewish, and only loosely observant. But as a kid I never questioned that Jewishness was where I came from and belonged. So I learned the

Hebrew alphabet, and could bumble my way through prayers and texts. I even came to know many by heart, including the Torah portion I was to chant on that day when I had turned thirteen. (I no longer participate in Judaism as a religion, and only now observe its practices such as lighting Hanukah candles occasionally, and sentimentally—and in effect socially. I do still appreciate the sense of belonging.)

Our next door neighbor on Drummond Avenue was Joe Mendelson, an Orthodox Jew who volunteered to tutor me in preparation for my big moment. My parents acquiesced, considering it an honor or else just not to be rude; it was a generous offer. Or maybe they asked him to do it, so they didn't have to pay some other scholar. Joe, perhaps because he was childless, and awkward with a kid, seemed remote and severe. That impression was enhanced for me by the strangeness of having to learn to sing for ten minutes something incomprehensible; I only recall him teaching me to memorize the melody and the Hebrew text, without any discussion of how it would translate or what it might mean. The process was excruciating, alleviated only by the plate of home-baked cookies his wife Martha would set in front of us at the end of each session. Confusingly, the Mendelsons had a little dog called George, and though by that age I should have outgrown this, I often would momentarily mix up their household with that other one that included a George and a Martha—the Washingtons, I mean.

The prayer books used by our Conservative synagogue had the Hebrew texts, plus phonetic transliterations so that people could more or less mouth along to the Hebrew without actually knowing it, as well as English translations. But even in translation, the liturgy's language and meaning were opaque. Its references were anachronistic and incomprehensible. Who, just for example, were these despicable Reubenites, Gadites, Danites, Gileadites, Naphtalites, and so forth, to whom we were obliged to direct our withering condemnation? I had no confidence that any useful lessons were to be found. Still, a sense of connection and comfort came along with uncritical assumption of this inheritance. The dolorous memorized laments of our forefathers were chanted to tunes which seemed to have been within me since before consciousness or even birth. Very little has ever made me feel more connected than that moment in the service when the congregation as a whole bows and then immediately raises its collective head and voice in a quick shift from minor to major key, like sun breaking through clouds. It didn't require an ability to translate, let alone explicate, the text to feel enfolded. I did want to feel enfolded.

This was surely my motivation for joining the Zionist youth group Young Judaea, when I was in high school, and for spending a month each summer during my high school years at its camp in Upstate New York. Doing so greatly expanded the abstract, buoyant self-conception of being part of a people. The organization provided community, camaraderie, friendship—*chevrut*, one Hebrew word I've not forgotten. I certainly did not grasp the conflicted implications of Zionism, vis-a-vis Palestinians for example. Zionism was depicted cinematically as brave pioneers making the supposedly empty desert bloom; Europe's stereotypically pale, weak Jews would develop muscles and deep tans. At that camp I learned more of the language and memorized more of the prayers, Israeli folk songs and folk dances too. I became able to decipher a slightly larger fraction of their literal content, but I still was mainly just reproducing the sounds, mechanically as a music box. That I hardly knew what I was saying in Hebrew prayers or Israeli folk songs left me quite untroubled. The feeling of belonging was what I sought and got. Craving for community was, similarly, why I later committed myself to leftist activism, and much of the rhetoric I absorbed and spouted back then might as well have been the devotional chants of some arcane religion in a language I could pronounce without comprehending.

At that camp, during the summer before my senior year at Hawthorne, I also had my first experience of sexual intercourse with a girl. You know, fucking. "How come you came so soon?" she asked afterwards in a small voice. This was troubling. She was frustrated, and I was deflated. Her question made unavoidable my cluelessness, not that I was concerned with how it had been for her. I muttered something breezy, and phony, like, "Oh, I always do," allowing as how without exactly saying so that it hadn't been my first time. It *was* the first, though there would be plenty more mediocre sex with girls—mediocre for those girls no doubt, and mostly so for me, too. I was sixteen. She was eighteen, more experienced, and into me. I didn't force myself on her. I just forced myself to make use of her, to score. The next day I tried to feel accomplished, catapulted into maturity, but I didn't actually feel very good at all. I knew something was wrong. Even if I'd heard of performance anxiety, which I hadn't then, I wouldn't have wanted to ponder why I had experienced it.

* * *

I loved cars when I was a kid, not their workings but their looks, their bodies. Back then cars were restyled or at least given some altered exterior flourish every year. Each September, I waited anxiously for the new models to be revealed. I can still recognize the make, model and year of most of those voluptuous fifties and sixties jobs. Their symbolism of technological power and mastery of the skies seduced me. Functionless vent ports and air scoops. Hood ornaments shaped like jet fighters. Front bumper guards aimed forward like missiles, and tail lights like cones of flame from afterburners. The models had names like Sky Hawk, Jetstar, Firedome. In the late 1950s, Chrysler Corporation's products arrived with "Forward Look and Flight Sweep" styling, marketing speak for raked-back windshields and enormous fins, and had automatic transmissions shifted by push-button, effortlessly, the way bombs are dropped. I didn't play soldiers as a kid, and don't have a uniform fetish as an adult. Still, I was perfectly comfortable with this latent martial imagery. (The other, obviously sexual, signals of this styling didn't enter my consciousness until later.) I was aroused by it to pride even, since our American military superiority was simply assumed, god-given, like our perfect democracy and our amber waves of grain. Or as I first misapprehended the lyric, in elementary school, before I could have grasped the implication of my garbled phrase, our amber wanes of grace.

Once, in Taipei, when I was ten or so, I was for some reason spending the afternoon at my father's office. He gave me pencils and paper and sat me at an unused desk. I entertained myself by drawing "The History of the Tail Fin." This schematic started with a rendering of the prepubescent bumps on the back fenders of 1948 Cadillacs and then depicted the progressive engorgement of these stirring but useless appendages through the ensuing decade. It was like those illustrations showing "The Progress of Mankind" in evolutionary stages from hunched-over dumb chimp to upright sapient chump. I ended with a sketch of the 1958 Packard which actually had two sets of fins, one on top of the other. That's the year when Packard went bankrupt. Delicious irony: You can give it winglets but you can't make it fly. But I couldn't have known of that corporate failure at the time, since it still was 1958; anyway, I didn't yet traffic in irony. I showed my drawing to Daddy proudly. He didn't react. Or, didn't react sufficiently. Another little wound.

Unlike me, he wasn't into cars as expressions of potency and desire, or status. Not then anyway. After he retired he and Kathy mostly drove Volvos. That was when a Volvo telegraphed restrained good taste and commitment to safety, more than luxury, rendering serial Volvo ownership a smugly unostentatious form of ostentation. But when I was a kid his choices of car were functional and budget-minded. Twice he bought used Plymouths decommissioned from the fleet of his friend who owned a taxi company. Both were a flaccid pale blue, as if to emphasize their blandness.

Having that Studebaker when I was sixteen years old was like sexual empowerment. *Like* sexual empowerment, a boy's delusion not the real thing. (I should say a male's delusion since the equation "car equals potency" continues to trick plenty of men old enough to have gotten over it.) The car transported me into a simulated adulthood requiring no tedious trial-and-failure acquisition of knowledge or maturity. This was abetted by a lack of parental oversight. That was not just due to my mother's illness and then absence and my father's distance and preoccupation, but also to the fact of American cultural history that nobody then, or nobody I knew, was subject to what's now called helicopter parenting. So sometimes I ditched school to wander instead through the National Gallery of Art. Sometimes I hit the road, like the night my friend Daniel and I on a whim cruised north three hours to Philadelphia, had pie and coffee at the twenty-four-hour Horn & Hardart Automat, and returned home at dawn. The car provided real mobility, and also let me try out alternate, or multiple, personas. Tuesday I could be a searcher after art, and Wednesday a vagabond traveling aimlessly—while Thursday afternoons and Saturdays I drove dutifully to my part-time job doing odd chores and deliveries for Claire and Joe's shop.

You'd think having the car would be enough to satisfy my adolescent itch. But I couldn't resist comparing my car to those of my friends. This is metaphoric behavior (though I must ask my brother and sister the psychologists if it has a proper term of art) since adolescent boys can't stop themselves from measuring the size, shape and other attributes of their bodies against those of their peers. I wasn't afraid of my own body, despite being insecure about my sexuality. But I mostly thought other kids' cars were cooler than mine, which fed my need to use, or should I say recklessly abuse, my car in compensation. But most kids I knew didn't have cars specifically for their own use. I can think of only two others who did, and they also attended private day schools distant from home which didn't provide bus transportation. But almost every kid I socialized with had access to a car often enough because almost every family in that suburban place owned more than one.

To me, some of the others' cars were cooler because they were foreign, compact in size and rational, if quirky, in design. These qualities embodied a critique of boorish American excess, an attitude inspired by the Beats and already fashionable among kids like us even before the more articulated countercultural sensibilities and ideological leftism of our later-sixties college years. Japanese cars had barely appeared in America, so these eccentric foreign cars were European: rear-engined Renaults, teensy Morris Mini-Minors, Saabs with two-cycle motors like those of lawnmowers that required a quart of oil poured into the gas tank at every fill-up. They implied non-conforming, cosmopolitan sophistication, as if we who could be glimpsed riding in them were the sort of people who wore berets, read Camus, smoked Gauloises, and listened to moody jazz. Actually some of us were reading Camus and smoking Gauloises, when we weren't reading Salinger or Kerouac, and smoking Luckies or Kools. Indeed, we were listening to moody jazz.

But some of the others' cars were big muscular American jobs, which had a different appeal. Daniel, who—embarrassingly, though I played along—nicknamed my Studebaker "the Rutabaga"—and his sisters Debby and Susan came from a family that had one car from each category. Which was the more seductive? They had a boxy Volvo 122, an austere but sturdy vehicle made in small-d small-s democratic-socialist Sweden. It was the first car I ever rode in that had shoulder safety belts. It had a four-on-the-floor transmission, which you only saw on foreign cars then, and was equipped with a sort of canvas window shade in front of the radiator that could be let down by releasing a chain on the dashboard, meant to keep the engine warm in frigid Scandinavia. The family's other vehicle was more Santa Monica than Stockholm, a Buick Invicta convertible with a 325 horsepower engine and tail fins canted outward at a forty-five-degree angle suggesting imminent fiery departure from this planet. Hard choice: the exemplar of discreet, efficient, morally and intellectually superior European design, or the dumb musclebound American road rocket aching to explode? If I'd had to be monogamous I probably would have committed to the Buick. I strove to be sophisticated, but my need to appear sexy was even stronger.

* * *

In 1960, when I was in seventh grade, the civil-rights-movement tactic of the sit-in was being employed with enormous courage in cities across the South, and even nearby in Baltimore. Typically, Black college and sometimes high school students would take seats at whites-only lunch counters. This would elicit at least consternation and more frequently violent reaction from white bystanders and the police. The sit-in closest to home was initiated by students from Howard University that June. It was at Glen Echo Amusement Park, Washington's main fun fair. The seats they occupied were not lunch-counter stools, but the saddles of wooden horses and camels on the carousel.

I knew Glen Echo well. Especially when I was small, it held an irresistibly terrifying fascination. The rides had names like The Whip and Tilt-A-Whirl. They were mostly designed to scare you, and toss and bang you around until you felt so giddy that you might throw up. My principal love-hate relationship at Glen Echo was with the Laughing Lady. This obese mechanical personage was positioned inside a slightly elevated glass booth so that she loomed over you. She was right next to the trick mirrors. These distorted your reflection, so that you were already feeling untethered from reality when you saw her. When you fed in a coin, she would rock forward and back for a minute or two, to a sound track of berserk laughter. Delicious scary nightmare material all, but since the park's opening in 1911 available to white kids only.

Glen Echo was just half a mile from Bannockburn. A month earlier, the annual meeting of the Bannockburn Community Association had unanimously adopted a resolution decrying segregation at the park. Spurred by the Black students' sit-in there, Bannockburners mounted a picket line in support, outside the park's gates, every subsequent day that summer. The neighborhood's kids formed their own steering committee and maintained a separate picket line; soon they started to picket as well at a segregated movie theater in Bethesda. (This wasn't the Deep South, and while there was some taunting by rednecks, victories were pretty bloodless. That fall, the theater was sold to a company that welcomed all comers. Glen Echo was integrated upon opening for the following year's summer season.) I didn't picket at Glen Echo, although I knew the demonstrations were going on, and I never again went there as a customer. But in the summer of 1960, when I was going into eighth grade, I hadn't yet made friends with anybody from Bannockburn. I only started to know some of them once school reopened that September.

Bannockburn kids tended to be smart, arty, ironic, savvy about jazz and folk music and foreign films, and always in the know about the next civil rights action. With them, and sometimes solo but inspired by them, I took my first steps as an activist, joining the picket line at a segregated apartment complex near where I lived, and a canned food drive to support a Black community in Mississippi that was boycotting its local white businesses. We were motivated not by ideology but morality: a simple instinct for right and wrong, the ethos we had absorbed from our liberal and mostly Jewish families, and from the unassailable dignity of the nonviolent movement for racial equality. Toward the end of the decade, when the Vietnam War was raging and attacks on Black activists were escalating, I started calling myself a "professional revolutionary" and joined that violent leftist splinter group. To my knowledge none of those Bannockburn kids ever made such a grandiose and supposedly (or as one might say now, performatively) political leap.

My parents had attended one or two of the early meetings where the proposal for the Bannockburn residential cooperative was discussed. Perhaps Abe and Elsie found the idea, or some of the initiative's leaders, unnervingly leftist. And I imagine my parents dreamed of raising their family in a less spartan house than those being envisioned, which indeed they managed to do. They had a perhaps more middle-of-the-road, less political and intellectual, idea of themselves. But once I made friends in Bannockburn, I resented that my folks hadn't stuck with it. I could have grown up in Bannockburn myself! From where we lived, three miles away, it took nearly an hour to walk there, but I did that anyway, numerous times. By bus, you had to go into the city and transfer to a different line back out, and it wasn't any faster. Once I could drive, the trip took less than ten minutes. But even then, I was jealous of kids from there, such was my craving to belong to something that felt elevated and uplifting and distinctly cool. This was of course irrational, since nobody there ever made me feel unwelcome just because I didn't live next door. And not living in their neighborhood had not prevented my becoming a part of their social circle.

I have the real estate itch, perhaps inherited from, or in emulation of, my mother. I still scope out properties for sale, though online now mostly—it's another form of internet porn, and possibly just as addictive. I'm still drawn to modernist architecture. But I live today with my husband Peter in a historic district, in an 1870 house that we renovated considerably. When the contractors were gone and we finally settled in here I swore that I would never move again. Our home is handsome and comfortable, and by now we have mostly made peace with its creaks and peculiarities. We're acutely aware of a few regrettable decisions we made in fixing it up. They're irritating as a pebble in the shoe, though hardly anyone else notices them. But Peter and I are house whores: we're always eager to get inside other people's places to imagine how we would redo them to suit ourselves (and to sometimes snicker sotto voce at dumb choices the actual owners have made). Both of us as youngsters wanted to become architects, and didn't. But each of us did build a design-oriented career, he as a photo stylist for the home furnishings industry and I through my magazine writing. Now and then we go through spasms of considering a move. If we ever make one, it will be mainly for the pleasurable challenge of shaping another place to fit ourselves, and trying to get it entirely right this time. And I at least won't be motivated by envy.

And why should I have envied the kids from Bannockburn? Growing up—in high school, anyway—I had plenty of good, even close, friendships, including with some of them. I was encouraged by their social awareness, and eagerly joined in their activism. With them I enjoyed foreign films, folk music, jazz, live concerts of the Motown Review and the Rolling Stones, picket lines for racial integration, and in the humid Washington summer refreshing, frosty glasses of Coke in a glass with ice, or gin with tonic or bitter lemon. Objectively, there were reasons they might have envied me. I lived successively in several nice houses, each by some measures grander than theirs. By age eleven, thanks to our move to and subsequent return from Taipei, I had traveled literally around the world, via ten countries, seventeen flights, two ocean-liner crossings and uncountable extraordinary moments. From eleventh grade I attended a school in many ways cooler than the huge conventional education factory where I'd been their classmate. At sixteen, I had a car to use at will. Maybe they actually envied me, I don't know. But envy is more about your relationship with yourself than that with other people.

My longing for belonging would appear to have defied satisfaction. There I was, a rising *macher*, or bigshot, in Young Judaea which attracted almost nobody from Bannockburn's overwhelmingly secular milieu. This gave me a second quite distinct social circle. And then I changed schools, so that while I stayed close to kids from Bannockburn and continued in Young Judaea, I effortlessly became a member of yet a third group, consisting of my new Hawthorne schoolmates, which had just about zero overlap with either of the other two.

I mean it when I say "I effortlessly became a member" and I can see the irony, that I should still have felt insecure while being easily welcomed by not one but three groups of peers. Paradoxically, I now understand both my craving for acceptance and my joining multiple, mutually exclusive social sets as underlain by the same fear. What if I were inauthentic—not worth knowing, not seen as fully a guy? Was I thinking of each group as a form of insurance against the other, against my being discovered, and uncovered—metaphorically left standing naked? I'm pretty sure that most, if not all, adolescent boys experience similar fears. The specific challenge for me was to hide the possibility—the fact— that I am queer. I didn't fully embrace being gay until decades later. Most boys don't have that particular anxiety, since most boys aren't gay. But surely most adolescent boys worry about being judged. Even if they are quite untroubled about their own sexual orientation, even if nobody is bullying them, the source of that trepidation is sexual: What if what they don't know about sex, and their own sexuality, is revealed? Boys can't escape being imprinted with the idea that feeling capable and empowered about sex is central to authentic adulthood. Actually, many boys tend to see it as more central than it necessarily is. Some guys never get comfortable with it, at any age. Self-doubt about sex compels many—gay or not—to try proving themselves, in ways often regrettable and sometimes despicable. Me, too, as a matter of fact.

4

Chain Bridges

I have been sorting through a pile of thirty-five milimeter slides taken by my father. When we lived in Taipei, he was moved to capture the exotic vistas and circumstances of our life there, so he bought a camera and started snapping. He was not a particularly good photographer, but I'm glad he did that. The images reinforce my memories of the place. I see myself in those photos as self-confident, and unselfconscious. I was happy there. I liked wearing colors (and still do): a bright red shirt and matching socks, or a shirt in fierce burnt orange with a brown, batik-like pattern. I also seem to have had a penchant for white shoes (which I certainly have lost). I am pictured wearing a pair, not sneakers but white leather loafers, in numerous photos taken on our long trip home from Taipei: at a roadside in India playing with some monkeys, en route to Agra to see the Taj Mahal; at a Tel Aviv corner with Mom, waiting for the light to change; in Paris, with her and my brothers at the base of the Arc de Triomphe; in a deck chair in the middle of the Atlantic, on the ocean liner Queen Mary. I was eleven when we made that trip. I had not yet experienced junior high school, or ever been taunted for my wardrobe choices or my enthusiasms.

In Taiwan I had grown a bit chubby, a fact of which I was blissfully unaware. The evening we arrived back in Washington, we were met at the airport by our closest family friends, adults and kids, fifteen or twenty people. The first thing everybody said on seeing me was, "Look, Jonny got fat!" They all came back to our house with us, and my pals and I went up to my room on the third floor. I sat down, or more likely flounced down, on the bed. It immediately collapsed under me. The kids fell out laughing, and repeating the observation that I was a fatso. This may have been the first moment I was ever made to feel self-conscious and ashamed of my body. I had always been assured by my mother, and her mother and other relatives, that I was a beautiful boy. It never occurred to me to doubt it. Really, at age eleven on arrival home from Taipei, I was hardly fat. That didn't stop me worrying about it for the next couple of years and even adopting a mild version of the binge-and-purge eating disorder more common to young girls. Then, with puberty, I grew tall and slim, and have remained so ever since.

Once we were home, Daddy's photo opportunities became more like those any suburban father might have chosen, special occasions mostly: parties, picnics, trips, graduations, various of us dressed up for important events. There's one of Mom wearing a simple floor-length sheath of dark periwinkle blue silk, and a string of pearls. Elsie and Abe were going to a wedding banquet—of Cissy's son, the first child of their inner circle to get hitched—and long dresses had been specified. Mom is posed next to the baby grand piano in the two-story living room, standing a quarter turn to the right rather than facing the camera head on. After her first bout with cancer in 1954, any time she was aware of being photographed she made an effort to hide her right arm. This was subtle enough to go unnoticed in the moment but is unmistakable when noted in slide after slide. It was easier to manage in a group shot, when she could step slightly behind someone else—one of us kids, usually. Turning to the right was the strategy for pictures like this one, of her alone.

Her cancer treatment had been radical mastectomy, a blunt and primitive-seeming procedure rarely used now which included removing lymph nodes. As a result, her arm swelled. Evidently, swelling resulted from half or more of radical mastectomies. For some women, it was a passing problem. At a doctor's suggestion I suppose, Daddy rigged a contraption, attached to the wall above their bed, that would hold her arm up vertically while she slept, to help drain the swelling. It didn't work, or maybe she couldn't bear using it; as I recall, it looked like an instrument of torture. Her right arm remained swollen for the rest of her life. Here was another secret in plain sight, more visible than most perhaps but still never discussed.

I notice, as I write, that I refer to my mother as Mom and my father as Daddy, or occasionally as Abe, but never as Dad. When I was little, I called my mother Mommy. As I grew older I must have felt that continuing to call her that would be self-infantilizing, undermine my transition into adolescence, and belie adolescence as a state of proto-adulthood. My instinctive usage now of Mom but not Dad—and Daddy but not Mommy—seems oddly inconsistent. Dad, after all, might be more comfortable, given the coolness of my relationship with him. Maybe I can't let go of "Daddy" because I still long for warmth from him that I did not experience as a child. But I don't think any of us four kids ever called him Dad to his face. We often called him by his initials, A.M. for Abraham Max, and since his death, among ourselves, we still do. I say "dad" now sometimes, when referring to him while speaking with anybody else, but even that rarely, and more often say "my father," which is even more distancing.

* * *

That day Mom died, when I went home to tell Higgy, the house was quiet, and empty. I guess Rebecca, our Black dayworker maid, was off. No one else was there. I was standing in the living room when I heard Higgy let himself in at the kitchen door. "Hig," I called, "I have to tell you something." He came through and asked me what. "You have to be strong," I said, an admonition which, of course, conveyed it all. He turned—twisted, really—and stamped into our parents' bedroom, just because it was beyond the nearest door, I guess. "Mom died," I felt compelled to say as I followed him. We ended up facing each other—why?— in the walk-in closet. An empty floor-length sheath of dark periwinkle blue silk hung there among her clothes. Higgy's body was clenched, his fists so tight they were vibrating. He cried, just a little. Did I say anything else? Did he? Did I hug him? No, I think, and no, and no.

This is the memory I have long carried. But now that I am unearthing memories, I realize that while it is not entirely wrong, it is not quite accurate or complete. That scene with Higgy did happen. But I did not drive myself home. I must have left the blue Studebaker at the hospital for Steve. I went instead with my future stepmother Kathy, who drove her car. I sat in back with my grandparents. Ida wept quietly but irrepressibly the whole way. Steve's girlfriend Marsha was up front with Kathy, also occasionally sobbing. She and Steve had met when they both took a gap year after high school to go on Young Judaea's "Year Course" to Israel, where they picked up a good deal of Hebrew. I had learned some of the language, too, at summer camp, enough to say to her the equivalent of, "We need you to be strong."

To be strong, as I understood it at the time, was to suck it up. And demanding this, playing the role of he who insists on suppression of feeling, made me seem to myself quite grown up—pulled together, self-contained. It was, after all, a replication of the behavior of my father, the nearest available model of an adult man.

After a while Steve, Marcia and Daddy arrived home. Maybe Mike came with them, and then maybe he and Kathy, on their own way home, took my grandparents to the airport. Daddy was at his desk, up on the gallery, where I could see him from the living room below, when he answered the phone. The caller was the mother of Marsha, Steve's girlfriend. Daddy assumed she was calling with condolences, but she had not yet heard that Elsie was dead. Instead, she had a bizarre piece of news: her husband, Marsha's father, had unexpectedly dropped dead, on the golf course, of heart attack, that same afternoon. My father's immediate reaction was a loud, short, violent cry. Like a bark.

Perhaps he cried at some other time, or in some other way, for the death of his wife, the mother of his children. But I never saw it. Meanwhile, the surprise of Marsha's dad's death gave us all something else to focus on.

Now it occurs to me to imagine what might have been different that day, if I had been at school in England, at Summerhill, as Mom had once suggested might cure whatever was ailing me. My father, if my portrait of his self-absorption and unconcern for the impact on us of our mother's death is correct, may not even have been the person to make the phone call to tell me. He would have had Marcia do it, probably. Or perhaps have communicated the news with even more emotional distance by sending a cable; sending cables was something Foreign Service Officers were used to doing. Would he have summoned me home, to the bosom of my family? People didn't just jet across the ocean like it was nothing back then, and in his calculation the cost and logistical challenge would likely have come first. Anyway, summoned me home to what, since there was no more opportunity to grieve there than I would have found thousands of miles away among strangers.

* * *

Mom's parents and her brother and his family lived in Hollywood, Florida, about fifteen miles north of very-Jewish Miami Beach. We visited them a number of times when I was a kid. During these stays we would usually take a ritual drive south on A1A, the coast road. It traces a long chain of barrier islands now densely and depressingly built up, with highrise condominiums that are beginning to crumble and collapse. Back then, it was mostly wild—just ocean, sand, scrubby palmettos, and beach grasses bent in the wind—until the sparkly hallucination of Miami Beach's postwar towers loomed up ahead. Possibly for my parents this pilgrimage was magical simply for placing us momentarily in a visibly, predominantly Jewish environment. We would stop for pastrami sandwiches, and cheesecake, or whatever, food overly rich but ethnically evocative and irresistible, at famous Wolfie's delicatessen.

But for me the allure was the architecture, even when I was quite young. Those hotels were the unhinged, flamboyant *beau idéal* of a modernism quite contrary to the hyper-rational and economical designs of the likes of Donald Lethbridge or the Bauhaus. And uncritically, I loved them just as well. This was Forward Look and Flight Sweep styling rendered in high-rise concrete and glass, all parabolas and *grandes jetés*. Beyond these newer towers were the smaller but equally, dazzlingly overwrought art-deco buildings of the resort's earlier decades, in the area now called South Beach. Buildings aside, I was enraptured by the hotels' names. Some happened to also be the names of cars, like El Dorado, Plymouth, and Cadillac—for me, a double thrill. Others were named for romantic-sounding foreign destinations: St. Moritz, Deauville, Casablanca, Fontainebleau (always pronounced "Fountain Blue"), Balmoral, Barcelona, Algiers. Just seeing these names in swooping neon made little-boy me feel cosmopolitan, luxuriating in assumed sophistication. Which of course is exactly what these names and this aesthetic were intended to do. When I was small it gave me not a moment's pause that I didn't know the first thing about any of those places. I thought incorrectly that they must all be beach resorts in France—France, in my mind, being the locus of *ne plus ultra* worldliness.

The last time I made a family visit to Hollywood, Florida, was soon after my high school graduation, in 1965 when I was seventeen, the summer after Mom died. It was only my father, Higgy, and me. We were staying not at our grandparents' or uncle's but out on the beach, at a hotel called the Thunderbird, the name of yet another seductive car. We didn't make the pilgrimage to Miami Beach that time. Mostly I recall that it was punishingly hot, and the puny air conditioning in my cousin Suzy's Corvair, which we had been lent, barely helped. One night I took myself, alone, into the hotel bar, and ordered a gin fizz. That's what my Bannockburn crowd at home called the icy highball of gin and Schweppes Bitter Lemon which we were guzzling that summer. Steve had given me a duplicate of his draft card, which when flashed would let me pass for twenty-one, but that evening nobody checked my ID. What I was served in the Thunderbird's dreary cocktail lounge, a space not quite as pretentious as I was in entering it, was a sloe gin fizz. I'd never heard of sloe gin. Sloes are intensely sour, barely edible plum-like stone fruits. Gin is infused with their juice and then made thick and sticky and supposedly potable with sugar syrup. The drink was awful, but I didn't want to appear unenlightened or phony, so I gagged it down. Another unsatisfactory attempt, another instance of faking it, in order to feel grownup.

I was hellbent on escaping childhood.

* * *

In my first term at Hawthorne, when the school was still located in that disintegrating townhouse, I spent a number of afternoons a few blocks down the street at the central library. I was doing research for a paper on social conditions precipitating the Russian revolution. Being new at the school, I was determined to be serious and do a great job on this paper. That library, a grand Beaux Arts structure which opened in 1903, had surely been beloved and bustling for decades. But by the mid-sixties the surrounding area was run down, and the library almost spectrally empty of users. This made it quiet and distraction-free, an excellent place to study. I certainly had no idea then what my life's vocation was to be, but in memory this is the first time I see myself *being a writer*: alone in a still place, watching dust motes, considering sources, waiting for ideas to form, getting them down in quick bursts, fiddling with my pen, watching more dust motes and then working the passages over, and over, and over. That's still my basic m.o.

I don't mean to say I was the only person who visited the central library in those days. I encountered another in the men's room one day. He was standing at the next urinal masturbating. I had already glimpsed this activity in bus station restrooms. But those were busy places, where discovery and exposure could happen in an instant. Certain men's rooms like these, and also those of department stores and highway rest stops, were and perhaps still may be common venues for this particular manifestation of homosexual desire, or desperation. As a kid, it was strange and alarming to see—though when I was older, in the sexually wild seventies, it was more common, and came to seem unremarkable. This time, at the library, with nobody else around, I couldn't ignore the bleakness of the practice, nor the thrilling and scary possibility that something could happen. Just theoretically. Between him and me, I mean. Although it did not.

Library men's rooms and bus station men's rooms were the first places I saw men if not exactly inviting each other to have sex in the moment, then furtively revealing and regarding each other sexually. It was both fascinating and repellent. This was different from the games my little boy pals and I played, when secrecy was fun. These were grown men for whom indirection and deniability were a strategy to avoid potentially lethal danger. Something related and similarly cloaked by the anonymity of travel could even take place not just in the station men's room but on the bus itself.

The first time I myself had sexual contact with a grown man was on a long-distance overnight bus trip. A few years earlier, when I was maybe thirteen, I had made a visit alone to my grandparents in Florida. I traveled there by bus from D.C., a trip of some twenty-four hours. In the night, as we rumbled along some stretch of U.S. highway, in South Carolina let's say, I was groped by the man seated next to me. I didn't exactly like it, but I didn't hate it. I was confident that no other passengers were paying attention. So I let it happen, the ick factor being overtaken by my curiosity. We were fully clothed. It was just rubbing. He didn't even open my zipper. Soon enough, out of nervousness, I climaxed. No words were exchanged. When he got off the bus, at Brunswick maybe or Jacksonville, it was still dark out and I pretended to be asleep. I felt queasy. But it was not much harder to dissociate from this incident than it was to pretend to ignore the men's room exhibitionism. I didn't forget these experiences, and they occurred repeatedly over the next few years, including similarly being groped on another overnight bus trip. But I didn't contemplate them, or examine the fact that, weirdness aside, they exerted a certain attraction. Still, I managed to act as if they had nothing to do with me.

Only one physical encounter with another guy during my high school years stands out for not being anonymous. It was regrettable for a different reason. I was on an out-of-town visit with my Young Judaea friend Mike. The two of us had grown extremely close. That night, we stayed up so late talking that we fell asleep together on a couch. Then we woke up and, while pretending we were half asleep, as I recall it, we made a sort of love. Cuddling, maybe even kissing. We were clothed, but nervously once again I climaxed. I knew Mike, knew I loved him and that he loved me. Unusually, we had actually expressed that, out loud. "I had this romantic notion, which I suppose I still have, of male love," he wrote in an email, when we reconnected recently after fifty-nine years. He reminded me that we used to talk about the ambiguous love story of David and Jonathan, in the Bible, as something to emulate. "That seemed idyllic for me. It was never sexual, just deeply emotional," Mike wrote. I surely intuited even then, on the morning after, that Mike isn't gay, and of course I was still fighting that idea about myself. What we had done left me feeling confused, and angry, and guilty. Maybe I thought he had led me on unfairly, with so much talk of intimacy. Or maybe he thought I had entrapped him. I feared he would despise me. I wanted it to go away. So I promptly ended our friendship, before he could— ended it cold, without saying a word. "I often wondered, in later years, why we lost touch," Mike said, adding, "I always remember you with love." It's no surprise that we recall that night differently. I remember it happening without our speaking. He remembers that I asked for more and that he replied, "I love you but I can't do this." I don't disbelieve him, but I'm surprised—proud, actually—that I might have been brave enough to voice what I wanted, even if I wasn't strong or clear enough to unravel how his wanting something different made me feel. It's OK now, still a wistful memory but no longer a painful regret.

* * *

The Hilltopper, Western Junior High School's yearbook, includes deer-in-the-headlights official school photos, at thumbnail size and dozens to a page, of each of the many hundreds of students. It also has awkward, posed group portraits of the sports teams and after-school clubs, though the 1961 edition, which I just realized I possess, does not include mention of my ephemeral Gourmet Club. Nor is there a photo of the cross-dressing boy cheerleaders. If I saw such a picture now, I hope I would smile kindly toward my confused and pained young self, rather than wince at the memory of humiliation.

Western's yearbook was many pages, perfect-bound in heavy boards covered in school-color-green leatherette. I also have Hawthorne School's yearbook, *The Scarlet Letter*, from 1965 when I was about to graduate. It, by contrast, is a fifty-page, saddle-stapled paperback, more pamphlet than book. The photos in it, candid and self-consciously arty, all shot by students, range from very good to truly incompetent. Even after I had forgotten I had this artifact and had not looked at it for decades, I recognize every picture, good or bad, though I can't call the name of everyone in them. I was on the yearbook committee. I had handled all those photos as we selected them, and I had helped lay out the pages. That was my first experience in publishing at a time when I imprecisely thought my future was in visual arts or something theatrical like lighting design, and long before I understood that my profession would be writing about how things look, not making them look that way.

I also helped write the yearbook's minimal text. The most salient thing about that, it strikes me now, is its total lack of cynicism. Trickled through the book and among the photos, in brief phrases and stanzas, it reads, in its entirety:

> *Once there was a stone and glass building. It*
> *had a big center. A lot of people lived there*
> *sometimes.*

They moved in

circles

    and patterns

The most wonderful thing about the building was

that everyone discovered something new in it.

and met

wonderful

people

(Here, the narrative pauses for three pages with photos of the twenty-six faculty members. Each is captioned with a fanciful name such as Lewis Carroll, Mack the Knife, The Farmer in the Dell, or else a name of a cartoon character of the era.)

and

each

    other.

They read and talked and laughed and studied and

made things . . .

(Here, fourteen pages of unposed, moody or funny and—for me, anyway—strongly evocative shots of everyday scenes around school; these photos are uncaptioned.)

and

had

time

to

be

quiet.

Each day, they assembled in the

center. They talked (and listened

sometimes) and then, like sparks

from a firework, went their own ways.

Protons

and electrons

of thought

flew through
the air.
They circled
and dived
and collided
and new atoms
were formed,
and the
people changed.
(Now come eight two-page spreads, each with six infor-mal portraits of us seniors, forty-eight in all, identified with our real names.)
Their images were reflected in the glass of the
building, which held them, and then reflected
the images back on the people.

I have been paging through this book, savoring again Haw-thorne School's exuberance, its idiosyncratic student body and challenging curriculum, and the extraordinary modernist build-ing in which all that was contained. Western Junior High's build-ing, by contrast, was a conventional suburban school of the fifties, sprawling across its hilltop with long dull facades. Inside were dispiriting windowless hallways and enclosed stairwells. It makes me think now of the urbanist critic James Howard Kunstler's indel-ible remark, "We build schools that look like insecticide factories." That school's yearbook, with its rigid and unadventurous layout, could have been designed by the same aesthetics-challenged tech-nocrats responsible for the building. Many schools built in ensu-ing decades are much worse, though; Western's classrooms did at least each have a bank of windows that opened. Still my sense memory of the place is of claustrophobia and suffocation. But I was mostly unhappy there for the first year or two, until I found that I had made some friends.

For tenth grade, I was at Walt Whitman High School. It was new that year too, which may sound impossibly coincidental, but schools were being thrown up all over the place in those years, in suburbia anyway, to accommodate us, the multitudes of the baby boom. These were also the years of the Space Race, and while Whitman's architecture was hardly iconoclastic, it did include a few of-the-moment gestures. In plan it was laid out, explicitly, like a rocket ship: the long main building was complemented by two short wings angled off one end, like fins. And instead of a conventional gymnasium we had a "Geodesic Field House," a vast dome of the sort promulgated by the era's celebrity-futurist architect Buckminster Fuller. I never heard mention, by the way, that the school's namesake Walt Whitman was a faggot and cultural subversive; I only learned that years later. A junior high in the same neighborhood also new that year was named, in the triumphalist spirit of the times, for a famous World War II correspondent, Ernie Pyle; now, that was more like it.

Looking through Hawthorne's *Scarlet Letter* is not unlike my recent Street View rambles through Bethesda and Chevy Chase, awakening nostalgia for the distantly familiar. It is a time capsule of the year when I was sixteen turning seventeen, and my mother was dying and then dead. I was desperate to pretend I was unscarred by that, and desperate to be what I thought of as a normal boy. I may have been a loudmouth, not entirely reliable, and frequently acting out. But at the same time, thanks to my skills of denial, I was engaged in and enjoying my studies and the life of the school. I can't remember which phrases I contributed to that flowery yearbook text but I realize now that I myself was not then a cynic. I was not, quite yet, angry. Or, I was not yet aware of my anger, if only because the ways my mother handled her cancer and my father handled her death had been a crash course in not allowing myself to have uncomfortable feelings, never mind expressing them. And I had learned that lesson well.

* * *

On the Hawthorne yearbook page, there sits Betsy. She is bent over and concentrating She has a lit cigarette in her hand. Betsy had a glamorous way of blowing out smoke sideways past her lower lip. There was something intimate and caring about that, as if she was protecting you from it, although a lot of us were smokers then, too, including me. (I smoked Lucky Strikes in high school and college, and the distinctly more butch Camels later when I joined the revolution. But always unfiltered ones—Luckies and Camels didn't even make filtered versions then. I'm not a fairy! How could you think that? I smoke unfiltered cigarettes!) Betsy, I discovered yesterday thanks to the all-knowing Internet, died of lung cancer just five months ago. The obituary I saw includes a photo in which she looks beautiful and wise and embraceable. She was a therapist, and a Buddhist, and is survived by a wife and two daughters and their families. She lived just ninety minutes' drive from me. I wish I had discovered that earlier, and gone to visit her. She looks like somebody I would still want to know. But I think I never saw her again, once we graduated from high school.

A few pages on, there is Henry. He was one of the gang with whom I would sometimes drive out to Great Falls or some other beauty spot, to sit around drinking beer or that cheap Portuguese rosé that came in bottles of terracotta-colored glass as if they were hand-made of clay by barefoot peasants. Henry went on to Antioch College as did I, but we never crossed paths there because at Antioch half the students were always away on co-op jobs while the other half were studying on campus, and by chance Henry landed in the other "Div," the other division. The Antioch website lists him now among "lost alumni," which had me imagining all kinds of period-appropriate bad ends for him, like being picked up by a violent hippy-hater while hitch-hiking to California, or taking too much LSD and kayaking into the oceanic haze never to be seen again. But then another Hawthorne student I just spoke to informed me that he is alive, and well, and a distinguished professor of history somewhere out West.

The kids in these photos are as alive to me as if they were here in this room right now—alive in their sixteen-, seventeen-, eighteen-year-old embodiments, that is. I myself don't feel like a different person from the seventeen-year-old I see gazing off the page in half-profile. Of course, my young face in the picture is firm and unlined; we are wrinkled now, those of us still alive.

I'm wearing a possibly smug half smile. Had I just said something smart-alecky? I have on a pair of sunglasses the broken hinge of which I have repaired with a safety pin.

Now Charlie: Handsome with regular features and a thick mop of dark hair, he looks down and away from the camera. He always seemed troubled. I could be wrong, but I've thought he was gay, which would have been cause enough for moodiness in 1965. (I should know.) I think Dante, the art teacher, may have thought so too. Dante never tried to hide the fact that he himself was a homo, or maybe he had tried and given up because he was just too obviously a flamer, and could afford to stop trying to hide because Hawthorne provided him a safe enough space. Charlie's family was broken in some way the specifics of which I can't recall. A divorce? Those weren't so common then. A death? Dante always seemed to be hovering around Charlie protectively, or lovingly. Was he a family friend, simply trying to be avuncular? Or was he in love with Charlie? Charlie and I weren't really friends. I was frightened of the turmoil I sensed in him, and noting again now his good looks I'm pretty sure I was also frightened of being attracted to him.

Could Charlie and Dante actually have been lovers? That kind of thing did happen then as it does now, although in those days generally with lesser consequences or likely none at all for whichever person was in the position of power. We all knew that another of our classmates, a girl I won't name, was trysting repeatedly with the music teacher. Or, we thought we knew this. How we might have known it, or thought we knew it, I don't remember. We weren't scandalized, though, just curious. And perhaps impressed—it seemed like such a worldly, grown-up thing, an affair with an older man. Well, I suppose I should speak for myself. Perhaps some of the girls, and possibly even some of the other boys, were less intrigued than I. More recently, I heard from a Hawthorne schoolmate about a couple of other girls known and/or suspected of having sexual relationships with members of the faculty, including with Sandy, the headmaster. He supposedly took one of them to a hotel, twice, but for naught: she refused to have sex with him.

But speaking of sexual force fields between teachers and students, and Hawthorne School's enabling underside, there's more about Dante. At Hawthorne, seniors had an option to "major" in art or music. I was an art major, which meant spending several hours each day in Dante's studio. I was oblivious that he might be attracted to me. It's not that I categorically found teachers unappealing. For example, in my inchoate way I fantasized about the smokey-voiced, buzz-cut, fireplug of a French teacher, Jean, despite the fact that he was married and his wife had just given birth to their first kid—I didn't fantasize sex with him, just some indistinct physicality. But Dante, who was sloppily overweight and gave off an air of dissipation, aroused me not at all. So when the day came that he kicked me out of class, declaring that he "simply could not be in the same room" as me, I was surprised. It felt unfair. Today his ejecting me from class like that would be nearly as unconscionable as if he had physically tried to seduce me. But I pretended I didn't care. Hey! Now I get two free hours every morning! I never discussed the matter with anyone on the faculty. Then on the day of our graduation Eleanor, the headmistress, informed me that while I was expected to go through the ceremony I was actually not graduating. My diploma would be blank, because I had stopped attending art class. That I had been kicked out didn't seem to matter. The so-called resolution was that I had to make some paintings over the summer, to satisfy Dante. It occurs to me that I don't know if I ever did technically graduate from high school. The school has been defunct for decades now. Its records are gone. There's no one to ask.

And suddenly I'm remembering another moment of emotional outburst at me by a teacher, Bruce Lewis at Western Junior High. One day, unnoticed by me, he overheard me making fun of him. I think I was joking about his hairy forearms and wrists. I called him a baboon or something like that. Furry forearms are a physical feature of masculinity that appeals to me as an adult. I suppose in a latent way it must have done so as a teenager as well, which makes an interesting subtext for my so-called joke. Later that day, he pulled me out of another class, seething with anger.

"Don't mock me!" he hissed, looming close over me in the otherwise empty hallway. I'm not taking issue with his being angry, or letting me know it. But his intensity frightened me, and seems out of proportion still. And then I'm thinking about those experiences on nighttime bus trips. Was I unconsciously signaling my sexual orientation, even before I understood it, in some way that was legible to these men?

* * *

Patti's yearbook photo mostly shows the top of her head; she's bent over studying something. Patti was the only Black girl in our class, which also had one Latino and two Black boys: four persons of color out of forty-eight seniors. That was approximately the ratio for the whole student body at Hawthorne, and it may have been higher than the ratio at huge Walt Whitman High in suburban Bethesda. I suppose Patti is the Black girl I once took on a date. I don't remember particularly liking her, or expecting that we would have sex which surely we did not, nor for that matter anything of substance about her. I just know I took out some Black girl from school one time, and can't think who else it might have been.

I do clearly see myself, in the Air Force Blue Metallic Studebaker Commander, pulling up in front of this girl's house, a row house in the city. I sat chatting with her parents while waiting for her to come downstairs. Perhaps, I now realize, they were trying to determine whether it was safe to let her go with me. I suppose they asked what my father did, what my college plans might be, and where we were headed that evening. That's another thing I'm blanking on. It must have been to some party or public event where people I knew would witness me escorting a Negro young lady, rather than to the anonymity of a restaurant or the invisibility of a darkened movie house. I was slightly taken aback by the interview with her parents. What little I recall of the conversation is suffused with awkward, genteel restraint. I didn't get that there were good reasons why they should want to know who this white male stranger might be, which reveals how superficial my grasp of race was. In today's jargon, since I wasn't really interested in Patti—or whoever the girl may have been—my taking her out was performative. It was a way to show off my supposed ease in crossing the color line, my laudable moral fiber and progressive politics. It could also be called by that other current term for the hollow and self-serving gesture, virtue signaling.

My grasp of race was superficial—not insincere, just lacking subtlety and dimension.

The apprehensions Black people might have about encounters with white people, such as the damage white males could possibly do to Black females, surely don't lack subtlety. Such scenarios may not have been top-of-mind for these parents, whose daughter had simply been invited on a date by a classmate from her safely liberal private school. Quite reasonably, they might only have wanted to get a sense of me. Like, was there any reason to think I would be a careless driver? I often was, but I guess I concealed that fact successfully. I certainly was aware of, and instinctively abhorred, the history of slavery and racial discrimination. But I saw the problems of racism as mainly originating in unfair laws, and the solutions as legal, too. Let's just call this understanding incomplete. I may have been capable of imagining the psychological ramifications, or even the inescapable everyday tediousness, that racism creates for Black people, and in less acute ways for everyone. But I had never tried, or been challenged, to think deeply about it.

* * *

Nancy was my best friend at Hawthorne. She had long red hair and wore lots of chunky Southwestern jewelry; she had spent most of her childhood in New Mexico. At sixteen she understood with certainty that she was an artist and indeed that's what she went on to be. In our senior year, she and I were on the yearbook committee together, and while I recall myself as tentative in proposing page layouts, she always seemed to know what would look good and never hesitated to say so.

We also worked together on the production of a play. That was an extremely gloomy piece called "The Misunderstanding," written in Nazi-occupied France in 1943 by Albert Camus. An elderly woman and her daughter run an inn in an obscure mountain location. To finance their dream of going somewhere less dreary, they murder guests and steal their money. The son, who has been lost to them for twenty years, during which he became rich, returns with the aim of supporting them. When at first they don't recognize him, he gets the bright idea to keep his identity secret for a bit just so he can observe how they are after the long separation. Naturally, they kill him too. Hawthorne School's students had a penchant for the tragically intellectual, or do I mean the intellectually tragic? I was the stage manager. Nancy designed the set which consisted mainly of some raw planks and olive-drab burlap, and an austere wooden table and straight chairs. It wasn't beautiful, but it well evoked the grimness of the story.

Nancy's older brother Peter, who didn't drive, was a student at Antioch College, which is in Ohio. He needed to get back to campus, so Nancy and I drove him there. This was early enough in the school year that we seniors had not yet applied to colleges. Nancy was desperate to go to Antioch herself. I'd considered it, because of its reputation for being different—the "co-op" work-study program, for instance, had been pioneered there and at the time was still quite unusual—and for having a student body of activists and beatniks. The college had got national press a few years earlier when students picketed the local barber who refused to cut the few Black students' hair. After Nancy and I hung out there for a few days with her brother's friends, who were arty and fun and mostly obviously queer, I felt perfectly at home and decided it was the college I wanted to attend. Antioch promised the kind of safe space I'd sensed at Hawthorne School, but with the queerness closer to the surface. In the end I was accepted there, while Nancy was rejected. She was crushed.

I did see Nancy a couple of times in the years after high school. Our last contact was when she called me, sometime in the nineties. She spoke in a breathless and insistent way about starting a Redhaired Gay People's Liberation Front. It seemed pretty wacky, and I thought, ungenerously, that this was a friendship I might not need to renew.

I searched her out recently online, only to discover that just recently, within days of Betsy, she too died. An obituary said that Nancy taught yoga and meditation, another echo of Buddhist Betsy. Betsy's obit had revealed that she was a lesbian, and I already knew that about Nancy. They were friendly at Hawthorne, and I wonder if they stayed connected. I want to think they did, perhaps to make up in a convoluted way for the fact that I let them both go out of my life so easily. (As if it's all about me.) But maybe those are all just coincidences. Nancy's obituary also explained that she had struggled for much of her adult life with bipolar disorder—thus that weirdly urgent last phone call is explained. The obit included a photo of the girl I knew, many years older and looking it, but instantly recognizable. She still had fabulous long hair, though now its red was shot through with gray.

* * *

My date with Patti (or whoever that Black girl was) would have been around the time of Bloody Sunday, March 7, 1965. That's when a peaceful march for voting rights in Alabama was savagely attacked by police. The gory televised footage evoked passionate reaction. This prefigured by fifty-five years the cell phone video of George Floyd's murder-by-cop in Minneapolis, and while it didn't provoke such enormous, widespread, and angry mass demonstrations across the country, it did bring people out. In D.C., a round-the-clock picket line formed at the White House the next day. It grew in numbers through the week. On the Tuesday, Jim Reeb, a Unitarian minister and civil rights activist, well-known in Washington, who had gone to march in Alabama was beaten there by white thugs. He died on the Thursday. The word of his death rippled among the picketers, an especially personal blow to many because of his time in D.C. It felt personal even to me. Some of my friends did know him, and it is possible that I had attended events where he was present though if so I hadn't known it. This mourning impulse I experienced for Jim Reeb may be another instance of my only pretending to know or have experienced an important something, in order to be considered one of the group. Or maybe it was simple and honorable empathy. Or maybe it was a safely displaced way to spill the grief I had bottled up about my mother, dead less than three months.

By Saturday, the crowd protesting at the White House had grown to fifteen hundred people. The following day, when Alabama's governor had been summoned to meet inside the building with the president, we numbered fifteen thousand. A few months later, propelled by reaction to the Selma attack, the Voting Rights Act of 1965 passed with overwhelming bipartisan majorities in both houses of Congress. Alas, with that swift act of legal redress, any analogy to the responses after George Floyd's murder totally breaks down. The convulsions following that more recent atrocity raised consciousness of the country's racist underpinnings, but swift structural and legal change, in the polarized environment of the early twenty-first century, was hardly imaginable, and is hardly forthcoming.

I spent a lot of that week after Bloody Sunday on the picket line at the White House, skipping school to do so, sometimes staying late into the night. I was impelled there, for catharsis after the shock of what had taken place in Alabama, and for the cleansing bath in a movement that professed non-violence and love. It was fun to be there and gratifying to believe that being there amounted to doing something important, which it was. Walking the picket line also engendered a feeling of pilgrimage and atonement, thanks to the endless loop along the sidewalk, the chanting of civil rights ballads adapted from spirituals, the carrying of a placard—negligible in weight as that was—as if I were carrying something like the pain and hope of people who couldn't be present. I savored the morality. I liked the joining in and banding together, much as I had in Young Judaea. For me, whatever the context or politics, a big motivation was always for connection, for being part of something big. I would feel moral commitment and communal engagement again two years later when I dropped out of college and joined the staff of Students for a Democratic Society. I had those feelings even more intensely two years after that, in 1969, when I helped to destroy SDS and create the cult-like Weathermen, when the politics became a strident call for disruption and violence.

By then I did have a fuller grasp, or the rudiments of one, of racism in its political and psychosocial aspects. I no longer saw it as just a problem of unfairness thanks to bad laws. In fact the ideology of the Weathermen expressed something it has taken these many decades since to become at all widely acknowledged: that race is essential to American history and pervasive in our culture, and—significantly, because almost no other white people talked about this back then—that there exists the phenomenon we called at the time "white skin privilege." The fact that we understood these things analytically did not mean that as an organization or as individuals we had relationships with Black people that were deep, or meaningful, or especially honest. Building those is long hard work and not everybody cares to try, no matter what they grasp analytically.

It's curious to me now that I only recall going to picket the White House that March week either alone or with friends from Bannockburn, but not with anybody from Hawthorne. The Bannockburners grew up in an environment of leftish activism. Hawthorne was radical in its vision of schooling, which combined intimacy with a spirit of inquiry. That was an implicit critique of mainstream education, but primarily a cultural rather than political one. As students there, in contrast to what I mostly remember at the huge public schools, we felt seen and engaged, instead of nameless and alienated. Perhaps for most of my Hawthorne schoolmates this moderated any urge to act politically. Or maybe I just didn't realize or can't recall that some of them were picketing the White House that week too.

The following month, organizers from Students for a Democratic Society, were planning their "March on Washington to End the War in Vietnam"—the first national anti-war mobilization of our generation, which took place that April 17. They asked Hawthorne School to open its gym as a place for out-of-towners to sleep. This proposition was thrown out to the student body at one of our daily all-school meetings. I can imagine Sandy and Eleanor delighting to have us grapple with this real-world challenge. I'm one of those who was against it, which is odd given that soon enough I became a full-time activist in a movement largely propelled by opposition to that war, and an organizer for SDS.

But I knew hardly anything yet about the conflict in Vietnam. Nor had I adopted what I would learn to call—in leftist jargon, where the expression is usually uttered with an air of superiority—a world view, a unifying ideological belief system that would draw links, for example, between racism at home and war in Indochina. Fickle memory: Sometimes I remember stepping up to the staircase landing to offer my opinion, during that meeting in the Hawthorne School atrium. Other times it seems to me I didn't speak, but only thought something small-minded like, "It doesn't concern us. Let them find someplace else to stay." A majority of the students felt the same and we voted against extending the invitation. I didn't attend that demonstration either. Nor did I join another one that took place the same day. That was another picket line at the White House, but in demand of a different set of civil rights. I'd never even heard of that second demo until the other day when Eric, the queer historian, mentioned it. It was the first proudly "homophile" demonstration ever mounted in Washington, D.C., our nation's capital, my home town.

* * *

I say that the Bannockburn kids always knew the when and where of the next civil rights picket line or cool music event, and I may have a completely subjective sense of this but it's Debby I remember having that knowledge the most. Debby had dark eyes and a helmet of thick, dark hair. She was smart and enthusiastic, a deft satirist but not a cynic. She sat right in front of me in ninth grade English, so we had plenty of time to get to know each other, traipsing down the hill and back between the school building and the public library where the class met—though not so much while class was in session; off-topic socializing was hardly in Mr. Lewis' lesson plan. Debby often wore a collared shirt like a boy's button-up. It was block-printed with a big, squarish, vaguely African design in orange and gray. I remember it because I spent so many hours staring at her back, possibly to avoid catching Mr. Lewis's eye and being called on.

Debby organized us to go into Black Washington, to the Howard Theater to see the Miracles, the Marvelettes and the rest of the Motown Review. To the Bohemian Caverns, for the Modern Jazz Quartet and Thelonious Monk. And to the Cellar Door to hear Odetta, and to Uline Arena to see Joan Baez. Debby somehow found out about the Ontario Place, an earnest little corner "coffee house." Bearing no resemblance to the espresso bars of today, it was just a makeshift storefront venue serving burnt coffee from a big urn, dime a cup I think. There we heard gritty blues from Mississippi John Hurt, and from Elizabeth Cotten whom Debby invited out to Bannockburn to a party. Debby's taste in music was catholic, at least between the fields of rock, jazz and folk. She somehow was always the first one of us to know about new albums by the likes of the Rolling Stones, Miles Davis, Bill Evans, and Dave Van Ronk.

Her house was a place we gathered, thanks in part to the added attraction of her equally smart and quirkily entertaining brother Daniel, the same Daniel who drove with me all night in the blue Studebaker to Philly for a slice of pie at the Automat. (Their sister Susan was enough younger that she wasn't really part of our scene.) But a crucial element was the welcome we had from their mother, Laure, who seemed to think it was both natural and a pleasure to have a living room full of teenagers. She treated us as if we were grownups. And we were eager to be, or to appear, grown up. The summer of our high school graduation, Laure rented a cottage for a couple of weeks in Wellfleet, on Cape Cod, and a gang of us were invited along. It was a small cottage; we extras slept in tents on the lawn. Brooke, another Bannockburn kid known for his quick word play, was not with us; he had gone on his new motorcycle to Martha's Vineyard. Soon after we all got back to D.C. we heard that he'd died there in a crash. The evening we found out, it was on the driveway in front of Debby and Daniel's house where we gathered to mill about mute, that same driveway I stared at recently at the start of my rambles on Street View. It was to see

Debby that I first ventured back into the world, two or three days after Mom died. Debby was sick with mononucleosis at the time. I sat on the edge of her bed. She pulled herself up against the pillows and said, in a tone of simple, pity-free inquiry, "What are you going to do?" It is the only expression of concern I can remember any of the kids offering. (But surely that can't be true.)

* * *

So we experienced in live performance a range of the era's Black music, from R&B to cool jazz to acoustic blues, none of which in origin and idiom derived from the experience or heritage of kids like us. We were also drawn to folk singers whose repertoires, before the advent of the music now called singer-songwriter, drew mainly from white people's antique traditions, Scotch-Irish via Appalachia and the descendent genre bluegrass. That was no more expressive of our affluent mid-century suburban lives than gritty songs by Black singers about sharecropping, chain gangs and fights in rural juke joints. We didn't care. We responded to and loved and sang and played all of it.

Yes, I had my own guitar-playing, folk-tune-warbling phase; it was practically obligatory in those days if you had the urge to be admired. I was mouthing lyrics learned from records: seventeenth century Irish and English ballads, tunes about events in the recent past like the dust bowl and labor battles of the thirties, and blues. None was about anything my friends and I had directly known in our short, sheltered lives. But the music touched us in the place where we yearned for something else. Looked at one way, parroting lyrics I didn't quite understand was pretentious and inauthentic. On the other hand, one purpose of music—and storytelling of any kind—is to transport listeners to places they haven't been, and where they may not even know the language. And in doing so, to awaken empathy.

Rock music, and singer-songwriter which emerged from folk around the time I was in high school, did speak directly to us, and about us. Of course there were love songs, sweet or moody or tragic. But the most powerful music of the era expressed the independence, the anomie, and increasingly the anger we felt as our horizons expanded and a critique assembled in our minds of the world we were expected to join. We sang along at the top of our lungs to those songs when they came on the car radio. I can see us yelling into the wind the caustic, dismissive lines of Dylan's "Like a Rolling Stone," while riding in the 325-horsepower Buick Invicta convertible with the top down and Debby at the wheel.

If rock and folk-rock and singer-songwriter were ours, jazz, blues and R&B came from a somewhat foreign territory, the country of Black people. But that was a place with no border controls restricting access to tourists like us. The music itself was the port of entry. We were proud, and perhaps a bit smug, that we attended those venues where we were among the very few white people— the Howard, the Bohemian Caverns—just as we were proud of our participation in the civil rights movement. Despite this, we also felt entitled among ourselves to sometimes talk in "dialect," and to make casually racist jokes. That this was inconsistent with our avidity for an end to racial segregation, and with our appreciation of Blacks as a people and of Black music, did not occur to us. Or, if it did, we didn't discuss it. For white people, conversation about and understanding of racism were superficial then, certainly far more so than now. We did not challenge ourselves to consider its ramifications, or its operation within ourselves. And none of us had a connection of equality with any actual Black person. The ones we knew best were the women who cleaned our houses. Some kids had known their families' maids for years, so the relationships could be intimate—unlike, say, my connection to Mr. Hatton who occasionally chauffeured me to nursery school—but close or not, still they were relationships of imbalance. It was not difficult to decry racial discrimination writ large while failing to contemplate its living presence in our houses.

5

Secret Passages

I was chatting with my neighbor Shannon the other day. He's younger than me by several decades—and straight but not narrow, shall we say. He also went to a small private high school full of what he called misfits. What he meant was that some of his schoolmates were deep into drugs or trouble with the law. I said, "We were misfits but it wasn't about drugs. We were hardly even smoking pot." I didn't become a regular pothead or dabble in psychedelics until I was in college. And in an expression of a survival instinct that for me was rare as I entered my risk-loving twenties, I always avoided harder drugs. I often in those years put myself into political confrontations where I could get beat up by cops or right-wingers, and joined in conspiracies that could have landed me in prison, despite being frightened doing so. But I avoided smack, and angel dust, and speed, the common death trips of choice in the sixties and seventies. Before I ever heard it expressed in these words, I think I subscribed to that new age dictum that "my body is a temple." I was reluctant to trash the sanctuary. I could see the visible damage to faces and bodies those addictions wreaked. OK, I'm vain, too.

My friends at Whitman were misfits, and at Hawthorne we were misfits, and even refugees from places like Whitman when being a misfit there felt unbearable. But with us it was more cultural, and more political than what I think Shannon was referring to. More psychological maybe, too, such as for me from being gay. But the truth is that by the time I was turning sixteen, even while still at Whitman, I was no longer being bullied. It is possible that some of the straight boys, like me emerging from the scariness of puberty, were more confident now and so had less need to pick on other people. I certainly was no longer intimidated in gym class, which in junior high had been the bullies' main venue. By the time I was at Whitman, on the soccer field if a ball came within easy reach I would bestir myself to give it a kick, but otherwise I ignored the goings on. If anybody passed a comment I let it roll off my back. Then I finagled an assignment as a library assistant for an hour a day and got myself out of gym class altogether. And then I transferred to Hawthorne, where there were neither gym classes nor jocks.

I think I was luckier than some queer kids back then when survival entailed so much more secrecy and fear, or queer kids now in situations that can frequently be just as hostile. Somehow I had constructed a bulwark of self-assurance, or self-protective cheekiness. Getting good grades helped. My class background did too, having imparted the assumption that success for me in some form was guaranteed. More importantly, I wasn't lonely any more. I had friends, and we considered ourselves cooler than everybody else because we were intellectual and arty and political. Or maybe I was no longer picked on simply because I had grown taller than many guys—I'm six-foot-two, or was before decades of gravity wore me down a bit. Besides, I liked how I looked well enough, which given the generalized mass insecurity of adolescence was another source of confidence. I wasn't aware of acting fey, either; if I was, people had stopped pointing it out to me. I was even doing a passable job convincing myself and anybody looking that I was into girls.

So why bother to change to Hawthorne School? Academics was not the impulse, although I was bored with my classes at

Whitman. Hawthorne's pedagogy was certainly more inventive and engaging, but Whitman was in what was understood to be one of the best (and richest) public school systems in the country. I do not recall myself there as being *consciously* agitated about being gay, because I was fairly successfully denying the fact to myself. But I must have felt conflicted anyway, enough so to force the issue. And my mother was intuitive enough to recognize that I was in turmoil even if neither of us ventured to name its source.

Today people speak of safe space, meaning somewhere that's delineated and defined as welcoming to those who may have reason to feel threatened in the larger unregulated world. Besides such formally designated sanctuaries, for queer people much of the American landscape has become increasingly safe over the years of cultural and legal evolution since Stonewall in 1969 (and still is, even if that safety is under increasing threat). The country is stunningly more safe for queer people compared to the time of that first homophile picket line at the White House in 1965, four years before Stonewall, or the preceding years of brave, dangerous, and obscure lesbian and gay activism. At Hawthorne School I felt release, like a long exhalation, a weight lifting off. But I did not just drop the facade and suddenly own up to being gay. I didn't accept that I was. But if I had, admitting it publicly would have been inconceivable then, even though I was lucky enough to find myself in that *safer* space. Hawthorne felt safer, but not because the school was openly supportive of queers. I would say that, back then, if kids who were confused or in denial about their gender identities or sexual orientations had encountered a place announcing itself as "Safe for queers! Step right in!" most would have run fast in the opposite direction.

Hawthorne was welcoming because it was less competitive and rigid and condemning, more accepting of difference and idiosyncrasy. And it was intimate. You were known, which is different from being exposed. So it was safer for gay people without explicitly saying so. Indeed, it was safer for the totally nerdy and the socially awkward and the emotionally troubled, regardless of sexual orientation. It offered a feeling, a probability, of protection, though not quite a promise. And I felt an ebbing, a withdrawal of danger—although danger never fully disappears for queer people. Not even now, sixty years later, for a harmless, mild-mannered, senior citizen like me living in a place full of arty, sophisticated, and avowedly open-minded people. Still, that atmosphere, that hint of freedom I sensed at Hawthorne, though unvoiced, was palpable. It didn't have to be voiced. I knew it when I felt it.

* * *

John was tall, handsome, very smart, and very shy. He had lived in a neighborhood immediately adjacent to Bannockburn and grown up with those kids. We are the same age but he was a year behind me in school, so we really only got to know each other well when he transferred to Hawthorne for eleventh grade, when I was a senior. We traveled together that year, long car trips for a couple of unaccompanied seventeen-year-olds to make, it might strike you. But I had no mother and an uninvolved father and he had an absent father and, as he readily says, an unmaternal mother. We went where we pleased.

In the dead of winter we drove to New Hampshire, to check out a newly opened college, called Franconia. (For reasons I can't recall, we drove there in my family's other car which also happened to be a Studebaker, a yellow Lark station wagon.) Franconia appealed to us because it was supposedly in the unconventional mode of Hawthorne. The place went under in just a few years.

In the summer, in the blue Studebaker, we went to Cape Cod with Debby's family, and then on to Maine. Eve, my sister's former dance teacher spent her summers there on the coast near Blue Hill. (She had been briefly my own dance teacher, too, when I was following my friend Carolyn to Georgetown like a puppy.) I called Eve and, not to put too fine a point on it, invited John and myself to stay. Out of politeness, or perhaps out of sympathy for my motherless state, since she'd known my family for years, she said to come ahead. After one night, to get rid of us no doubt, she firmly suggested we go climb Mount Katahdin, clear across the state near the Canadian border.

We drove there, slept rough, and hiked to the top of the mountain the next morning without so much as a water bottle for equipment. We were, of course, invulnerable because we were seventeen. (Invulnerable John moved to the Northwest after high school and went on to be a serious mountain climber, acquiring the busted knees and other injuries to prove it.) From there we went on to Quebec, just to spend a night in a foreign country. I wanted to test out my high school French, and feed my idea that foreign travel, especially to a Francophone locale, was the essence of sophistication. We ordered omelets and red wine in a little restaurant that I remember, possibly too romantically, as having low ceilings, and stone walls, and drippy candles on the tables.

Oddly I can't remember what John and I talked about on these long drives, or that we even talked much. Can that be so? On some of these trips, because we were crashing at somebody's house or were economizing, we shared a bed. When he and I were back in touch not long ago, after decades, he told me that on at least one of those occasions I reached for him in the night. We were both wearing underpants. It was a tentative, questioning, scared invitation: my palm on his hip. He pretended to be asleep, and that was as far as it went. I didn't specifically remember this happening with him, but I do remember exactly that scenario with several other guys, over the following years when the voluntary poverty of radical activism often had people sharing a mattress. I piercingly recall the torture of lying awake with a rigid erection and making such potentially dangerous passes at guys who were my friends but uninterested in being my lovers. So there's no reason to doubt I did it with John.

His parents had divorced and by the time he was at Hawthorne he had moved with his mother Zilla to an apartment in D.C. Zilla also owned a splintery old cabin about fifty miles away at the foot of the Virginia Blue Ridge. Nowadays cul-de-sac suburbia spreads that far from Washington, but in the sixties it was the for-real country. The cabin—which I should probably render capitalized as The Cabin, so important was it to us all that we spoke of it as if it were the only rustic antique dwelling in those hills—may have dated from the eighteenth century. I suspect it had been the original house on a hardscrabble family farm, built as a single room-with-loft and later expanded with a second. It was far down a dirt road, set in a little shrub-tangled fold of land next to a run, as creeks are called around there. It was magical in many ways: an evocative relic of an (imagined) homespun past; an access point into what seemed like primeval nature (even if the present woods were second growth); a place to sneak off to alone for a day (instead of going to school); and a place to party with the gang.

We were all devotees of Edward Gorey, and often teased John by chanting the final line of Gorey's *Gashlycrumb Tinies*, which is an alphabet of ways to die: "Z is for Zilla, who drank too much gin." We all liked Zilla, because she was feisty—she would have had to be, having been a labor organizer in the South in the thirties, and still being what was then demeaningly called a "professional gal," working for the International Association of Machinists. She was unconventional, and we liked her for it. Not only did she have the cabin, her car was a Willy's station wagon. This vehicle, which lacked even a hint of creature comforts, was a direct descendant of the World War II Jeep. It had a four-wheel-drive system that only engaged if you first got down in the mud you were trying to motor out of and manually turned the wheel hubs. We also liked Zilla because she let us have the run of the cabin, which was another thing to make it feel magical. Of the many times I was there, I remember Zilla being present only once. That was at a big, raucous party during Christmas vacation of my senior year, some two weeks after Mom's death.

Losing a parent marks a kid with a scar that can make others uncomfortable, the way a glimpse of someone missing a limb might. In that era and at that age, when we didn't easily express feelings, I was pretty lucky. My friends surely felt concern, even if they expressed it only haltingly. Their awkwardness was probably relieved by my own affect, of appearing to shrug it all off.

A lot of people were at the cabin for that party. I suppose I got pretty drunk. Dave Van Ronk's album "Folksinger" was playing. I knew that record well and may even have been the one to put it on the turntable. It was close and hot inside the cabin. I stepped out to the narrow porch by myself. I remember it being a mild night, which isn't impossible in Virginia in December, but I may just have been overheated, or anesthetized with booze and not feeling the cold. The porch had no railing. I was sitting on its edge, my legs dangling off the side. I had left the door open, behind me, and could hear the hubbub and the music. The song "He Was a Friend of Mine" came on. It's a ballad, told in the first person, about loss and grieving and loneliness. The following track is called "Motherless Children." It's brutal, too, dismissive of the ability—or maybe the willingness—of fathers, and sisters, and even lovers to fill the empty space when a person's mother is dead.

Well. You can imagine.

I cried for a long time. People—friends—came out to see what was going on. I think a couple of them touched my shoulder, or knelt down to ask if I was alright. I was temporarily blind, though, so I couldn't really see them. Eventually I was drained. I felt the physical relief, the discharge of tension, that a good cry can produce. I didn't understand anything more, or differently. I wasn't any more able to say what I was feeling about Mom's death. But I pulled myself together and went into the kitchen, where Zilla and a couple of the kids were standing around. They all looked at me, their eyes full possibly of care, but also possibly of dread. In my memory, nobody spoke about what had just occurred, myself included. Maybe so, maybe not.

* * *

Because I'm closing in on eighty and nervous about—let's call it—mental slippage, I have been studying Spanish. I'm doing it to exercise my brain. They say learning a new language helps. I'm also doing it because Peter and I sometimes go to Spain on holiday. I love being there, and like to imagine myself striking up engaged conversations, such as with the random person on the next stool at a bar. (This doesn't work well. I'm not quite fluent enough, and I'm not gregarious enough to comfortably start chatting with strangers, even at home and in English.) I've also been reading contemporary Spanish fiction. I picked up *Sepharad*, by Antonio Muñoz Molina. It's about twentieth century European history: totalitarianism, the Franco dictatorship, the Holocaust, and their victims, focusing mainly on Jews and writers—subject matter in which I am more than mildly interested. It is also a family saga. I anticipated being affected by the book. But I did not expect it to speak to me this directly:

> *You will try in vain to remember the sound of her voice, for she stopped visiting you in dreams years ago. Again you are only guessing what she would have thought, the words she wanted to say to you but didn't have time, the advice that would have served you well, that might have kept you from making so many mistakes . . . Your face changes without your noticing, making you look like the person you were at four or five—and also the person you were when you were sixteen and your mother died. She pressed your hand on the mussed sheet of the hospital bed and said something you couldn't understand.*

* * *

Janet, one of my oldest and dearest friends—of forty-five years—had metastatic breast cancer and was close to dying. This is what killed my mother, and while the medical technology has changed quite a bit in the intervening decades, the durations and progressions of their diseases were remarkably similar. Last week, when Janet was brought home from the hospital, Peter and I jumped in the car and headed to Boston, to see her one more time. We were halfway there when I got the text: Too late. My first impulse was to turn around and go home. Maybe get drunk, maybe pull the covers over my head. Maybe both.

I sometimes feel as if I have secreted a shell. It must be transparent because other people generally don't notice it, but I feel it there. When something affecting happens, to me or to somebody I care about, there's almost always a time lag before I know what I'm feeling. My first response to many upsetting things is usually dismissive. I think, "Don't worry about it," which is a way of telling myself to not react, and a way to justify a delayed or stifled response or none at all. My supply of empathy for other people in pain seems to me small, or if not small then difficult to access or express. I have to intentionally dig for it, and then find a way to convey it. And I sometimes feel as if I'm only reciting scripted statements generically appropriate to the situation.

What accounts for my emotional reticence? Of course, it can't have a single origin. Becoming motherless in that exhausting and inexpressible way, with Mom's long undiscussed decline and then my family's inability to mourn—my father's ban on mourning—surely is a major component. All that provided effective training for pretending bad things weren't happening. Then, just because I'm gay didn't mean I could avoid being acculturated as a man in a culture that trains men to not show vulnerability. Being gay might give some people readier access to emotions or to mannerisms for expressing them. But being smacked down, as a child for gushing, even by strangers, surely helped shut me up. The time in junior high a kid on the school bus threatened me for using the word cute: "Don't let me catch you saying that again," he sneered. "That's a girl's word." The time in elementary school when a classmate's big brother and his pals told me I shouldn't be enchanted by the velvety texture and vivid color of a bed full of blooming tulips, because liking such things was for girls. And so on.

Perhaps I am making too much of my supposed emotional inhibition. Perhaps to the extent that it persists it is no more than a knee jerk, a muscle memory that expresses out of habit but doesn't prevent my feeling or showing what I feel. Maybe I am more emotive than I think, thanks to the wisdom of age, effective psychotherapy, enhanced self-confidence, and no longer giving much of a shit what other people—such as big boys, powerful boys or any other emotional cripples who might get in my way—should think of me.

* * *

I have very few things that belonged to my mother. Actually, these things belonged to my mother and father together. But she was the one who chose them—for "her house" as people used to say in those days and perhaps still do, the house being understood as the wife's domain. Like, "Elsie has a beautiful house." And in the case of my mother, the house(s) and decor, expressions of her taste, were indeed lovely.

One of the pieces I inherited is an altar table brought back from Taipei. It is in a handsome traditional Chinese style, though it's warped and missing bits of its fretwork. It turns out to be neither rare nor especially old; scores of virtually identical ones show up online, so my hunch is that they were factory made early in the last century. A pair of elegant Chinese candlesticks, tall and heavy and looking good on that altar table, turned out to be pot metal with a faked bronze patina. These faux antiques would likely have been bargains, the canny dealers in Hagglers Row letting them go cheap because they knew their paltry worth. Perhaps Mom let herself be fooled and took pride in thinking she had deftly snagged bargains, or maybe she doubted their authenticity but figured they were good-looking enough to impress anybody who would see them back in Chevy Chase. I also have of hers, from the defunct Washington department store Woodward and Lothrop, a tall, mid-century-modern, Italian glass lamp of a type that is now quite desirable, although this one is a middling example. I don't mind the imperfections of these items. These are the only things I possess that my mother actually touched.

Except, of course, for those vivid letters from Taipei, and some snapshots. One of these photos could have illustrated a feature titled "Housekeeping for Newlyweds" in a magazine such as *Ladies' Home Journal*. My mother is probably twenty-five. She is slim, which is not how I remember her, and very pretty. She's standing at a stove. Her cap-sleeved dress is a dark color, navy I imagine, with an all-over pattern of small pale blossoms. Over it she has put on a ruffly organza apron. She wears lipstick and, atypically, a small bow clipped into her curly hair. With one hand she has lifted the top off an aluminum percolator, and she stares down into it as if bemused by its contents. In the other hand, she is holding an open cookbook, perhaps hoping it might explain how to use this coffee-making device. She never much liked cooking.

The setting of this picture is a kitchen I never saw. It is either in the D.C. apartment my parents lived in when they were first married, or in the little house they then bought in Bethesda, ever after known in the family as "the bungalow." The bungalow was pointed out to me once or twice, but I never entered it. I always vaguely felt it unfair that Marcia and Steve got to live in it while I didn't because the family moved, to that house next door to Edmund Laughlin's family, around the time I was born. So the bungalow has a cryptic significance for me, an essence I can never know. Actually that's not unlike how I feel about my mother now. She is a person I can never know. Some sixty years distant, she has resolved into an assemblage of static photo images, blurry memories like fragmentary action clips, and those few minutes of her recorded voice. And those letters.

I had never seen this photo of young Mom in her kitchen until recently. It reminded me of another spur-of-the-moment jaunt I made in the blue Studebaker, in 1965, a few months after her death and that party at Zilla's cabin. It was a mild spring day. I suddenly craved irresistibly to see the ocean. I remember bumping into somebody in the school atrium and recruiting him to agree that we should immediately get the hell outta there. We cruised across Chesapeake Bay to Rehoboth Beach, two and a half hours away. I recall that the person who came with me was John, though he doesn't remember it.

We—I and John, or whoever—were sitting at a picnic table by the beach eating ice cream cones when at a distance I saw my mother. Not Mom as she had been in the recent past, gray and bloated and dying, but as she appears in that old photo. Svelte, pretty, vital, young—younger even than in the picture, like my age at the time, a teenager. I watched this person for a minute, looked away, looked back, and she was gone. "I just saw my mother," I muttered to whomever.

I hardly claim a lifetime of ghost sightings. Only Mom that afternoon at Rehoboth Beach, and those enslaved Africans at

Bremo. Her I wanted to see. I must have wanted to see them too. They were indistinct, passing through walls. But she was as if in the flesh, all there, smiling at some companion, unmistakably the young woman in the photograph, although I'd never glimpsed that photo at the time.

* * *

At Western Junior High School we had a form of sex education, which was called something like "Health and Hygiene," a title which immediately suggested its opposite, sickness and filth. These sessions, which were not co-educational, were conducted by gym teachers—not a group, if I may be permitted to generalize from my own limited experience, known for emotional intelligence, or pedagogical skills off the playing field. I remember we watched a dorky film about "good" boys contracting syphilis from trampy "bad" girls they pick up outside a burger joint. Debby told me that in her girls' gym class the teacher advised, "Don't get pregnant, or your breasts will invert," which aside from being absurd seemed to everyone, perhaps inexplicably, to confirm the suspicion that this teacher was a dyke. And I don't know what went down in other families, but the only conversation I ever had with my father about sex took place after I told him, in a way calculated to provoke, that I was not a virgin. I presented myself at his State Department office one afternoon, and announced, "You'll be happy to know that I have gonorrhea." "Christ," he said under his breath with a familiar note of exasperation. Then he said, "Well, now you know what women are for." It was the briefest of chats, and devoid of all advice beyond the suggestion that I see a doctor. (And as it turned out, I was imagining the gonorrhea.)

Did I stumble over the word *fucking* when I was a teenager and young adult because I knew I didn't actually want to be fucking girls, and couldn't wrap my mind around doing it with boys? *Making it,* as a euphemism, was cool and carefree, while as a descriptor it neatly captured the one-sided, penetration-and-orgasm-fixated, conquest-counting approach to sex that obsessed so many boys, including me. It happened to be the case that I was making it with girls in an attempt to convince myself and the world that I was not homosexual, not weak, effeminate, and mentally ill. Straight boys who were making it with girls probably only hoped to prove to themselves and the world that they were manly. Is there a significant difference? But even a boy who wasn't worried that he might not be sufficiently masculine or sexually "normal," and who was genuinely attracted to girls, was unlikely to have more than the vaguest understanding of the processes and potentials of sex, physically or emotionally. Nor would he be likely to have any more nuanced language to describe it. Our class in Health and Hygiene certainly didn't fill in those blanks.

I think that boys generally did not understand sex as communication, or give-and-take, or that it could encompass a spectrum of acts and opportunities. Possibly this is still true of most boys, and girls too. Still, in the years since I was a kid we have had feminism, and out-and-proud queerness, and improved sex education, and a cultural shift generally toward more open conversation and away from previously unmentionable topics. That self-centered, blindly groping, testosterone-driven kind of adolescent sex may be less pervasive now. Perhaps the kids have a more felicitous way of naming sex than *making it*. Of course it would be easy to wishfully overestimate the liberating cultural progress since the mid-sixties, especially now that it is under sustained attack and the forces of repression are winning major battles. And it would be a mistake to discount the powerful distortions of pornography, which is probably the main source of sex education for kids today.

Surely many, or most, teens of my generation were curious or even obsessed with sex. How could they not be, given puberty's hormonal imperative? But I also think that at the time many, or most, at least in the world I inhabited, were too scared or unconfident to try having any. A few were more daring, or mature. I knew boys who were not only dating girls but in long-term relationships that were sexual—pairs of junior grownups in love. My usual pattern was different. Once I'd made it with a girl, I ignored her.

Take kooky Carolyn, with whom in eighth grade I used to go to Georgetown to take modern dance classes. By our senior year she and I weren't at the same school any longer, or crossing paths much. But intelligence reached me that guys were calling her a nymphomaniac. I believe that slut is a more common term now for somebody—female or male—who sleeps around. (Although who am I to know what language young people use today?) But nympho carried a darker, pseudo-psychiatric implication of compulsion. It referred only to girls, girls who couldn't resist getting laid and didn't care who laid them. During the week of Christmas vacation that year I was home alone for a few days. This was two weeks after my mother's death, I will once again remind those keeping track and perhaps wondering if my father had at some point stepped up to provide succor to his kids, which he had not. And it was perhaps a couple of days before that party at Zilla's cabin when I cried. Steve was with his girlfriend Marsha's family in Upstate New York where, he later reported, the grieving for her father was fierce. Lucky him; maybe that helped. Marcia was back in New York City where she had lived since leaving home for college, and she was not alone; she was already seeing Ricardo, whom she later married and was with for more than fifty years. Higgy, I am pretty sure, although he describes those weeks as a total blank, had gone with Daddy to visit Cousins Pearlie and Leonard in Pennsylvania. Knowing that I had the house to myself, I asked Carolyn out on a date.

I took her to dinner at a Middle Eastern restaurant that had belly dancers. I thought it would get her in the mood, and she seemed to enjoy the show. At dinner, she was her familiar witty self. Then I took her home. We were drunk. She spent a few minutes woozily trying to replicate the belly dance moves we'd seen. Then we went to bed. There wasn't any conversation about it. It was all just physical moves. It didn't occur to me that any verbal intimacy—voicing of affection or care, or of requests—might be missing; this wasn't the first time I had intercourse with a girl, but was only the third or fourth. I fumbled mutely toward the goal of fucking and climax, baffled about female anatomy. I certainly didn't know anything about how to give someone else sexual pleasure, but that wasn't what I was doing this for. I wasn't really even doing it to give myself pleasure. It didn't occur to me that if Carolyn was as experienced sexually as rumor had it, she might have been able to help. But she didn't. She didn't say anything. Perhaps she was feeling mute despair: *God, not this again.* Or exhausted rage: *Him too! He's just another one . . .*

After we were done, by which I mean after I came, she started to weep. I'd never heard that this could happen. I asked her, "Why are you crying?" She murmured, "Oh, I always do." Always? I'd like to remember that I said something comforting but I couldn't have, because I only wanted her to stop crying and get dressed so I could drive her home. I had thought of Carolyn as a free spirit, confidently eccentric, even brash, maybe a bit crazy. Debby often called her "charming," but in a way that was at the least ambiguous, with a roll of the eyes. Everybody knew Carolyn saw a psychiatrist. But it never had occurred to me that she could be fragile. Of course I was habituated to avoid naming or discussing anything painful. And I only wanted to savor what I'd just achieved, disconnected as it was but which I thought at the time was the whole point: nonchalant fucking, another notch on my belt.

The custom with yearbooks, as with ours at Western Junior High, was to hand them around so your classmates could inscribe little rhymes and sentiments on the inside covers. Most of these ditties were embarrassingly stupid, accurately conveying the social awkwardness of that time of life. Some kids would turn to the page where their teensy mugshot was, and sign their name over the photo. I just now had a little shock when I looked for Carolyn's picture in our seventh grade yearbook. Someone has excised her image. It was done very neatly with scissors; no adjacent kid's image was even nicked. I am thinking that the culprit must have been myself. I don't think I even knew her until the following year, but perhaps I did this later, after we had made friends, when I fancied myself in unrequited love with her? In our eighth grade yearbook, her picture has not been cut out but it's completely scribbled over. Neatly, again: no mark strays onto anybody else's mug shot. I'm pretty sure that must have been her doing, in response to my request for her autograph. I can picture her obliterating her image while flashing me a mischievous smile to say, "I'm so wacky, huh!" It's disturbing now to consider what this episode could have revealed about the depth of trouble she was in, if anybody had been paying attention.

After that time we had sex, it's possible that Carolyn and I bumped into each other occasionally. But I'm certain I never again sought her out. I don't know if she's even alive now. The Internet doesn't seem to have a trace of her, but maybe she married and changed her name. I'm not thinking I would contact her, but it might assuage my guilty feelings if I could just determine that she is well and has enjoyed a good life. Of course, if I did find her, it might turn out that her life has been a disaster.

* * *

There was another girl I treated with similar shabbiness, a Hawthorne student. I barely knew her. I don't remember her name. I'll call her Joanne. She didn't have the charisma or quirkiness of the girl on whom I had once had a crush and whose genuine friendship I was willing to trash, the girl I've called Carolyn, whose real name I have never forgotten.

The summer after my graduation I asked Joanne on a date, to go boating. My family had a dorky little outboard cabin cruiser. In relation to other cabin cruisers it was as klunky and unglamorous as my Studebaker sedan was compared to more alluring cars. Still, it was pretty cool to have a boat. We kept it at a marina on the Potomac, near Memorial Bridge, that was usually deserted on weekdays. The boat had an airless cramped cabin with a pair of bunks tucked into the bow. I gather that during the several years after my mother died but before Kathy had managed to divorce Mike so she could marry my father, she and Abe used to meet there, on the boat, for trysts. I had no idea about that at the time. I wasn't trying to mimic him. This was a scenario I came up with all by myself, to add to my count.

It was a hot day. Probably I'd brought a cooler with some beers. I took Joanne out puttering around on the river for a while. We tied up somewhere, or maybe just came back to the marina, and I put the moves on her. Maneuvered us into the cabin and onto one of the bunks, and out of our clothes. As things proceeded toward intercourse—proceeded rapidly toward the endpoint fixed in my mind—maybe she said no, or maybe she said stop, or slow down, wait, or I'm not sure I want to do this, or something. And I probably said it's OK, or it will be fine, or don't worry, or something, but I did not stop. I mean, I fucked her. If she had resisted me more vocally, or forcefully, or strategically, it could have turned out differently. Hitting me would probably have worked, as I am a wimp; even just making fun of me could have been effective. But she wasn't forceful, which must be why I had her in my sights, since I wasn't really interested in her as a person. I can think of these ways she might have tried to get me to stop. I have no memory that she tried. Most likely she was, more than anything, scared. But I wasn't paying attention to her, or for that matter to myself. I was performing an act I had been given to understand—or had given myself to understand—that I had to do in order to be a normal, straight boy. To do what I did I didn't think about her feelings, and I shut down awareness of my own too.

There was no violence involved, but that doesn't mean there was no coercion. I had no formal power over her, as a boss, or uncle, or teacher, or priest might have had. I wasn't even older. But I was a graduated senior, bigger, perhaps seen by her as powerful due to my reputation for cockiness, or my pretensions to artiness, or my looks—or even just because I had a car and a boat although that last idea would especially demean her.

My mental picture of this encounter is suffused with heat and glare, shards of summer sunlight refracting off the water. Conjuring it up makes my eyes hurt as if poked with something sharp. I see us fucking, and see us afterward sweatily, silently getting dressed in the cramped, suffocating cabin, see myself driving her home. I'm sure I never spoke to her again. I also see now that she was a virgin. I see that because it's screamingly obvious, in hindsight.

She wasn't the only inexperienced girl whom I pressured into similarly awkward, probably undesired, and surely unpleasurable sex. And there were others not as inexperienced as I, whom I didn't need to urge on—they would do the urging— with whom I had sex once or maybe twice, but then similarly disregarded. What should I call these encounters? I am committed to the nuances of meaning; conversation and understanding are not advanced by dumbing words down. Can any of these acts accurately be considered rapes? Assaults? Those words connote violence and threat. My friend Paula was born the same year and grew up in the same cultural milieu as I, although we didn't know each other until recently. She has a strong sense of herself, and I'd bet she did at that age, too. She told me, "Girls then still thought we were 'dating,' and if it ended in a squirmy, uncomfortable, and shameful act, well, we just called it a 'bad date.' Later, once we got the pill, we could talk cavalierly about the range of fucks, from zipless to heartbreaking to just plain bad."

However you name them, these encounters can't be undone. According to an obituary, the writer Janet Malcolm, who died the other week, once said, "Autobiography is an exercise in self-forgiveness."

I'm working on it.

* * *

This next episode can't have been much separated in time from my shabby treatment of Joanne because it was during the same summer, and summer doesn't last that long, even when you're a kid and it feels endless. Why I wanted to have sex with a prostitute is only the first question I didn't stop to ponder. I guess the short answer is that I was just horny. But I also thought I wasn't getting enough, judged against my (unfounded) belief that most other boys were getting so much more. The longer answer might be that it would give me something audacious and rare—among kids of my background, certainly—to bolster my feeling of manly potency, and maybe even to brag about. Why I needed to rope my friend Frank into coming with me is another puzzle. I suppose it was a way of making this kind of score count: My daring would have a witness. It's also possible I was attracted to Frank, and proposed this escapade as a way to share something sexual without having to confront the idea, never mind the possibility, of actually having sex with him. I don't remember it that way, but there are subconscious motivations and that one is credible enough. Or maybe I was just scared to go alone. Why taciturn, retiring Frank agreed to come along is another puzzle. Perhaps he was reluctant to appear less than obsessed with getting laid, which would have left him no choice.

We went into D.C., to Swann Street, which every randy suburban white boy who'd never been there seemed to know was where you could pick up a whore. Swann Street was at the time a grim alley in the Black ghetto, not a place we would normally have gone, and for sure not after dark. Today, seen on Street View, all its little row houses have pretty paint jobs, and there are well-tended plantings along the herringbone-brick sidewalks. The sidewalks have surely been relaid in the gentrification that has made the neighborhood charming. A lot has changed in Washington real estate, although a surprising number of Swann Street windows are still barred.

Standing on a corner there we were approached by a pimp. How much, we asked? Ten and two. Huh? Ten dollars each for the girls, two each for use of the room. Frank and I didn't have $24 on us, but I had some cash at home. We drove out to Chevy Chase to retrieve it, and then back downtown. The girls he set us up with could have been in their twenties, but they just as easily might have been fourteen or fifteen. The one I was paired with said she was called Peaches. They took us down the block and into a house. We passed through a room where someone was sitting in the dark watching a TV with the sound off, and into a narrow second room, dimly lit, with one double bed. Frank has told me that he remembers thinking incredulously, "This is where I'm going to have sex for the first time?" Peaches declared jauntily, "I got me a white boyfriend!" as we were starting to undress. "Just take down your pants," she instructed. The girls only pulled up their skirts. Peaches turned her head to the side, lips clenched shut. "OK, you better hurry up and do your business," one of them ordered once we were lying down on top of them, both couples on the same bed. It was all over in minutes. Premature ejaculation had cut short all my early experiences of intercourse with girls; that had been disturbing when I was trying so hard to pretend intercourse with girls was what I should be doing. In this instance, I didn't much mind. I wanted to get the hell out of there.

I may have intended going with a prostitute to provide me with swagger material, but I only told one or two people about it, quietly. I didn't want to remind myself of it. It was too surreal and ghastly to boast of, even before the politics of the situation, the power imbalance, dawned on me years later: two well-resourced white boys, and two Black girls reduced to turning tricks, possibly to support drug habits, and to support that pimp—but why they were on the street is none of my business. Years later Frank and I met again, a fond reunion. Eventually our talk came around to this episode, which we had never spoken of to each other after the fact. He's still a thinker, and no longer so reserved. "I couldn't do it," he volunteered, unembarrassed. "I'd never had sex before. I couldn't get it up. I was glad it was so dark in the room, so you wouldn't know." I'm thinking how awkward that must have been for him to manage and, self-absorbed as I seem always to have been in these early sexual encounters, how oblivious I was to his experience of this fiasco. What looms most bizarre in his mind is the image of the person in the other room, watching the silent TV, in the dark.

* * *

Perhaps I wasn't the only person who thought of Debby as my best friend. She was—though in a mild and uninsistent way, which I think manifested her self-confidence—the center of that circle, the Bannockburn circle. Or, she was at least my strongest link in. And now, by putting it that way, I have evoked a dim but recognizable twinge of insecurity: I didn't grow up there, with them; did the rest of them like me, was I really accepted, or just a hanger on?

Debby had a vivaciousness that made her stand out. It was always curious to me that for many years after she and I had lost contact, both my father and my brother Steve—neither of whom probably ever spent more than a total of twenty minutes in her presence—would occasionally ask me if I ever heard from her.

I had never been attracted to Debby romantically or sexually. But then, that summer of our graduation, she got a boyfriend. This threw me. Now I can see that I was jealous and afraid, not of their romance but of losing her companionship. When I heard about their relationship, I drove over to her house, and sat down facing her as if to confront her, or plead. But all I could do was sit, in a spasm of muteness. "What? What?" she said. But I wanted her to read my feelings without my having to put them in words. *"What?"* This must have been puzzling to her, not to mention irritating.

But we *were* friends, and friends we remained during and after that short-lived romance of hers, and even during our first college years when we were hundreds of miles apart but wrote, and visited back and forth, and hung out together when we were both in Washington at holidays. When I turned eighteen, in 1966, during my first year at Antioch, I had to register for the military draft. The form asked for the name and address of somebody who would always know where I could be reached. Always? Of course! I filled in Debby's details. Once I dropped out of school and got deeply involved in the radical movement, we lost touch. After the Weathermen had become a clandestine organization devoted to armed action, in 1970, renaming itself the Weather Underground, the FBI was looking for me. Besides pestering members of my family, they went to Debby. She couldn't possibly have known anything useful to tell them even if she had been willing to do so. I don't know exactly how they harassed her. But a year later I went looking for her, and was told by her father that it had been a severely traumatic experience. I saw her just once then. She didn't want to talk about it, and later made it clear that she wanted nothing to do with me. I've never seen her since.

I have had no contact with any of the other Bannockburn kids either, aside from John, for decades. For my part, I guess that's another instance of my tendency to let people go. For their part, I suspect they may have been alienated by my deep dive into militance. That could seem odd, considering the leftish culture of the community they grew up in. My earliest introduction to activism, in the civil rights movement, was through my then-new Bannockburn friends, and Debby more than anyone. Here's the irony: What distinguished the founding ideology of the Weathermen from all the other factions and sects of the New Left was our obsessive (some might say delusional) focus on racism and Black liberation. We believed that Black people were on the verge of leading a violent revolution and that our role was to support them in doing so. Just because my old high school friends were in favor of civil rights and racial equality, and surely by then would also have come to oppose the Vietnam War, did not mean they would have had sympathy for my high-drama performance of subversive fervor.

* * *

I look through my Hawthorne School yearbook with wistful fondness, for the friendships I had there and did not maintain, and for the school's fertile, elastic culture which is so manifest in the book's design. It reminds me, too, of the illusory freedom of being sixteen, seventeen, with a car and with all of metropolitan Washington—and by extension, the world—spread out before me.

But I have a hard time looking at my yearbooks from Western Junior High. The feeling they instantly elicit is of confinement and mortification. Tiny student mugshots in grids of fifty to a page, each image less than a square inch. In gym class, when we had to do laps around the sports field, the teacher would run behind us with a switch and prod the stragglers, including me, on the thighs and butt to hurry us along. For my first two years there, I felt sick to my stomach every morning riding the school bus. I was lonely, an outsider. In the Webster's New World Thesaurus of 1971, which I keep on my desk, the word "belonging" is immediately preceded by the word "bellyache."

When I was miserable in junior high, it never occurred to me to regret having skipped fifth grade. But now I wonder how my adolescence might have been different, and possibly easier, if I had not. At the time, skipping ahead felt like winning an award. If we had returned to Taipei for a second tour, I would likely have been the youngest person at the junior-senior-high section of Taipei American School. But I expect that I would not have experienced the sort of shock I got arriving late for seventh grade at Western. My classmates would have been kids I already knew, from the year before. There was a gymnasium and a basketball team at TAS, but I don't think they bothered much with physical education. "It was just unsupervised mayhem, as I recall," says Steve, who was in eighth and ninth grades while we lived there. And the whole stripping-naked-and-showering-with-other-boys thing wouldn't have existed.

But we did not return to the delicious strangeness of Taiwan. So if I had not skipped ahead while we were there, once back in Chevy Chase I would have done sixth grade with the cohort I'd been in before we moved overseas. I would have attended the storybook red-brick elementary school one street over from Drummond Avenue. I wouldn't have needed to ride a school bus since everybody lived in the neighborhood and walked. From our house there was even a shortcut through a neighbor's back yard. The inevitable conflicts raised by puberty likely wouldn't have intruded on my life for another year, until I was in junior high. I wouldn't have been alone with them, and maybe I would have been more ready to handle them, and wouldn't have felt so threatened—or been so threatened. And longing for Taipei would no longer have been a depressant.

That two-year sojourn in Taipei seems in retrospect to be a bubble, a time apart, as if it is unconnected to the story I am telling. I certainly have not given it much ink here. It's not that I have forgotten it. In fact, I've written a novel drawing largely on my memories from there, so I spent several years immersed in those, and poring over Mom's letters and Daddy's slides. Still, it seems like a detour, as if nothing that happened and nothing encountered there affected or became throughlines once we were back home. Nothing except that we met the Birnbaums—Kathy and Mike and their four kids—and then my father and Kathy fell in love, and then our two families were disrupted and rearranged, and we are living with the fallout and implications of that upheaval to this day.

* * *

Another tiny photograph, this one two and a half inches square. It's a casual snapshot of my family, minus Higgy who would not be born for another four years. We are on a lawn, in our backyard perhaps. That would have been at the first house I remember, the one where Walkie and Talkie lived behind a panel in the wall and Edmund lived next door. This picture must have been taken in autumn, because the grass is strewn with fallen leaves. And it would have been in 1948 when I was about six months old, because I am in a metal bouncy chair and wearing a diaper. This was some special occasion—a Sunday afternoon visit from out-of-town relatives, perhaps?—since everybody (except me) is a bit dressed up. Marcia has on a tartan-plaid dress with white cuffs and Peter Pan collar, and a bow in her hair. Steve is in what looks like a little-boy suit of shorts and matching jacket, also with a Peter Pan collar, and sporty argyle socks. Mom wears a jacket thrown loosely over her shoulders and glamorous dark glasses, and Daddy has on a tweed blazer with shirt and tie. My parents sit right behind me, Marcia and Steve crouch close on either side. The shadow of the person who took the picture—that indelible signature of the amateur photographer—falls across the foreground. Off to the side, something amusing must have been happening because that's where Mom, Marcia and Steve are looking, all grinning widely. Daddy however is facing the camera with a firm handsome smile, holding his palms on either side of my head to make me face it too. To no avail: it seems that I insisted on looking wherever I wanted, which at that moment was down toward the ground.

How young and happy they all appear. My sister and brother are adorable. Those two are young enough to still perceive the world as a jigsaw puzzle with shape-shifting pieces, to believe magical truths such as putting honeysuckle blossoms in water overnight makes honey, even to still have imaginary friends. My parents are in their thirties, looking relaxed. I imagine them full of optimism. Their kids are bright and healthy. They have just bought a new car, the two-tone gray Buick Super we had until I was seven. Daddy's construction business will surely prosper. They will build that beautiful house of their dreams near Rock Creek Park. Mom's cancer is a tiny undetected cell only just starting to misfire.

* * *

I have not forgiven my father, and maybe I am not trying to. But I long ago stopped being angry at him. There's a difference.

He died, at age ninety, in 2001. The night before, I sat up with him, in his hospital room, by myself, until dawn. He was in a coma. But I'd heard it said that hearing is the last sense to go. So I talked to him nonstop, and sang every song I knew. In the morning I left to catch a plane, for a writing assignment on the West Coast. I didn't need to witness his final breath, which came later that day.

The following week, our clan—seven of Abe and Kathy's eight children, with our partners, the grandchildren and a few other relatives—gathered for a week on an island on the Florida coast. One sunset, we put Daddy's ashes in a little wooden boat and floated it out into the Gulf of Mexico. King, my partner at the time, had given all the women white handkerchiefs he had inherited when his own father died. They waved them from the beach in farewell.

* * *

How soon after Mom died did Daddy tell me he intended to marry Kathy? He told Steve after just two weeks. They were on the Interstate. Steve was driving. "I nearly went off the road," he says. At the hospital, when Mom died, Kathy and Mike were there with us, close enough friends to be the only people present who weren't family. So this information was startling. It took some effort to grasp, though possibly less for me than for my siblings; now I could make sense of that disturbing scene of my mother in misery, in Taipei, provoked by the Sunday night screening of *An Affair to Remember* at the Grand Hotel.

We all loved Kathy. She was irresistibly charming. That didn't mean we were elated by this news. When Daddy told me they were in love, I responded that if she were my age I would be in love with her too—an unlikely story, as my leanings in love would turn out to demonstrate. It was a statement I later wished I could unsay. Sure enough, he would repeat it now and then, with an air of jocular pride as in, "Hear what my smart kid said?" My father and step-mother forever after insisted that they hadn't *done anything* while Mom was alive. They'd simply been struck powerless by an irresistible force, but by superhuman effort had waited. I forget which one of my siblings or step-siblings first called it— later, and bitterly—*The Love Affair of the Century.*

Daddy told me his intention. It was childish in its simplicity, as was his confidence that it would unfold with ease: Kathy would divorce Mike. Kathy would marry Abe. Abe would take an overseas assignment. Life for Abe and Kathy would become an extended honeymoon in an exotic locale on Uncle Sam's payroll.

I was in my last months of high school. I had made that trip to Antioch with my classmate Nancy and her brother Peter, and liked the place. On the College Board entrance exam there was a question about what schools you wanted to attend, so I penciled in Antioch. I received a high score on that test, and soon Antioch invited me to apply. The only other college I had considered, for half a minute, was Williams. Sandy, the Hawthorne School headmaster, urged me to apply there. He thought I could use the structure. (He was right.) Traditional in its academics and at the time all male, Williams sounded as opposite to Antioch as could be. It scared me, not so much the implication of rigorous pedagogy as the all-male environment which would require again hiding my desire while surrounded by beautiful boys. I didn't take Sandy's suggestion seriously. But I hardly discussed the issue of where to go to college with anyone. This will sound bizarre to parents of today, but I had not a single conversation with my father about where I should study. I simply announced that I was headed to Antioch. Imagine how grown up that made me feel.

As summer was approaching, Daddy described the steps to their future that he and Kathy had devised. To divorce Mike, she could spend six weeks in Idaho to establish legal residence. Abe had let it be known at his agency that he wanted an overseas assignment, and had been offered a posting in Indonesia, to start in the fall. Marcia, Steve, and Kathy's two older kids, Ashley and David, were all out of the nest, but there were her two younger daughters, Debbie and Lisa, and my brother Higgy. They would be out of school for the summer and need looking after. Daddy proposed that when school ended in June, Kathy and I should load them into the yellow Lark station wagon and go out West, and that I should then accompany them all to Jakarta. I guess that in Idaho we would have stayed in a motel or a furnished apartment, not at a luxurious dude ranch as rich people and movie stars famously did back then when they wanted to divorce and the state they lived in made it difficult. To me this proposal seemed strange enough to be attractive. I saw myself at the wheel, accelerating along the swift, clean, new Interstate highways through an exotic part of the country I had only glimpsed in films. The faux-adult role I could play was appealing. So was playing that faux role alongside Kathy whom, conflicted feelings aside, I loved and enjoyed. A sojourn in the Wild West followed by Indonesia—and the pleasures of Foreign Service life—sounded fine to me. I don't think I thought about my dead mother at all during this time. And to this day I have no idea why my father wanted me to come along when they went abroad. As compensation for Idaho, maybe, or to be a baby-sitter. But I eagerly agreed. I called the admissions people at Antioch: Could I come a year late? Sure.

* * *

I have described my relationship with my father as brittle, and his attitude toward my siblings and me—toward me anyway—as swinging between indifferent and irritated. It's difficult to align that portrayal with how I know he was, and was seen to be, in social and professional settings. At parties he often provided the entertainment. He had a big laugh. He was an enthusiastic improvisational if not especially good pianist—there always was a piano in our house—and he compensated with zest for his keyboard slips. Often, when the party was somewhere else he would bring his accordion. People enjoyed having him play. His repertoire included traditional Yiddish tunes which, along with the charm of this being home-made music, warmed up gatherings of family or friends, perhaps even evoking some vague nostalgia for the old country which almost none of them had ever actually seen.

And in less intimate and homogenous groups, his playing could break the ice. There is a photograph of him, circa 1958, dressed in suit and tie and his heavy black-framed glasses, with a dreamy look on his face, playing the accordion. On the back, in fountain-pen handwriting as immaculately controlled as Chinese calligraphy, is this message: "To Mr. Lerner, Thank you very much for your wonderful contribution to the Christmas party for the psychiatric patients at N.T.U.H. [National Taiwan University Hospital]." It is signed by a Dr. T. Lin. There's another photo of Daddy from Taipei, sleeves rolled up, working with a group of volunteers to pack canned food collected for people left homeless by a typhoon. When Claire and Joe were set to open their first store, Joe told me many years later, they were in a panic to install shelves and racks. "Abe said, 'It's no problem. Let me just bring my tools over,' and he worked all weekend getting us set up." Claire, who sometimes and not inappropriately referred to herself as The Fashion Queen, once mentioned how well dressed he always was—which I really didn't get, because to me he was usually just wearing one indistinguishable business suit or another, but I figure she would have known. And Debby's mother Laure, who only met him once at a dinner party, at the home of her neighbor who was a colleague of his at work, remarked to me how much she enjoyed his company, and how handsome he was too.

As I have been working on this passage, the Hebrew mourner's kaddish has been quietly playing on repeat in the back of my brain. I just realized that today is his birthday. He would have been one hundred twelve years old. So much for my insistence that I am not subconsciously affected by important anniversaries.

I mentioned earlier the way he could mock gay men. But he did that without real animus. He was only echoing the ingrained homophobia of his era. And when I came out, he quickly let that go. It was in 1990, when I was forty-two. I called to tell him that I was leaving my wife of thirteen years because I was gay and finally had to embrace the fact. His immediate response, on the phone, was to say, "Well, you're good looking. You shouldn't have much trouble." Really, I had to laugh. For the next little while he was angry at me, but because I had been dishonest with my wife and was abandoning her. When I found King, my first gay "husband"—as we sometimes called each other, though this was long before we could legally have married—Abe and Kathy were eager to meet him, and welcomed him into the family. Some years later, when Abe was in rehab after a serious illness, I drove down to Florida to visit him. As I was leaving, he thanked me for coming and added, "Come again, son, but not without King."

In the years when I was in high school, he was Chief of Employee Relations for USAID, the State Department unit responsible for foreign aid (and for certain sinister clandestine operations as well). In that role, he often had to help individuals out of some crisis. He probably addressed personnel problems with logistical know-how more than empathy. I guess he had some ability to relate, though I doubt he would have been given a job like that today. He was not schooled in or patient with psychology—"Freud, Schmeud," he blustered dismissively to my two older siblings even as they both became psychotherapists, and each married a psychotherapist too. But more than once, for example, he helped arrange hush-hush abortions for female foreign service officers. The USAID employees he helped out must have appreciated his efforts because a number of times they left rather significant possessions with him for safekeeping while they were posted abroad. A Steinway grand piano was one. A 1956 Pontiac Chieftain and a 1961 English-built Ford, called a Zephyr, were two others. The Pontiac was a gray two-door sedan, the sort of lackluster but respectable vehicle that would have been perfect, in the sexist stereotype of the era, for a spinster librarian who kept her cardigan held tidily to her shoulders with a sweater guard. The Zephyr, which was the no-color of porridge, was a car with slightly more appeal if only for being imported and uncommon, and having a stick shift which was considered by kids like me to be the more authentic way to drive. Both of these cars had been retrieved by their owners by the time the Studebaker Commander came into my life. Come to think of it, the Commander could have been those two cars' love child. It was similarly frumpy. But it was mine, and I gunned its Sweepstakes 259 V8 engine and bombed around the Beltway as if I were in a drag race to adulthood.

* * *

If my mother had not died wouldn't our family—our nuclear family, the Abe Lerners, in the locution used by people of our time and place—have gone on intact? Had Elsie not already had cancer and her first mastectomy, would my father have allowed himself to fall in love with Kathy? He might have become infatuated, but would he have considered convulsing our two families so that he could marry her? My father did not routinely, or ever really, share intimate thoughts with me. Except this once, not long before Mom died. Out of the blue, he shocked me by saying, "Your mother doesn't think she's attractive to me any more." He said it very quietly and with sadness because, I imagine, it was true. He added, "But she's a wonderful girl."

How different our story, my story, might have been, if not for a single cell in my mother's breast that abandoned its normal behavior to spread out of control.

* * *

School ended for the summer. Kathy was not ready to go—Mike was threatening that he would take her to court for all their property and custody of their two young daughters. The road trip for a divorce in the West kept not happening. The six weeks she would need to spend there began to encroach on the start of the school year. Then it was August. My friends were getting ready to go off to college. Kathy had still not made the break.

One by one, kids I knew left for school. Indonesia became a chimera with no fixed departure date. For something to do in the meantime, I introduced myself at the Washington Theater Club, a scrappy venue now long defunct. They would let me volunteer as a production assistant. That would place me in an arty and presumably diverting scene. But it was also a frightening prospect: Wasn't it common knowledge that the theater world was crawling with homosexuals? Imagining myself in such an environment was threatening.

Debby was the last of my friends to leave for school. I went along as she shopped for a new winter coat. I sat in her Bannockburn bedroom as she packed a trunk. Then I drove home to Somerset in the blue Commander. I phoned Antioch and asked if I could enter in the approaching term after all. The registrar said, "Sure. Be here by Monday."

So I did my own shopping, alone. I bought my first pair of Levis, and a pair of then *de rigeur* Wellington boots. I bought a portable typewriter. I too bought myself a new winter coat. It was a hooded navy wool duffel with toggle closures and brown fleece lining. It was handsome but also functional. It would serve me as outerwear and also occasional blanket for years to come, when I became an activist-vagabond. I packed my own trunk and delivered it to Railway Express. Somebody drove me to National Airport, maybe my father but just as likely my brother Steve. The plane banked over the Potomac. First Memorial Bridge and then Chain Bridge passed below, as we climbed west into the clouds.